RESPECTABLE AND DISREPUTABLE

ALSO BY JEFFREY C. BENTON

A Sense of Place: Montgomery's Architectural Heritage, 1821–1951

The Very Worst Road: Travellers' Accounts of Crossing Alabama's Old Creek Indian Territory, 1820–1847

They Served Here: Thirty-three Maxwell Men

Air Force Officer's Guide (31st–36th editions)

RESPECTABLE AND DISREPUTABLE
Leisure Time in Antebellum Montgomery

Jeffrey C. Benton

NewSouth Books
Montgomery

NewSouth Books
105 S. Court Street
Montgomery, AL 36104

Copyright © 2013 by Jeffrey C. Benton
All rights reserved under International and Pan-American Copyright Conventions.
Published in the United States by NewSouth Books, a division of NewSouth, Inc.,
Montgomery, Alabama.

Library of Congress Cataloging-in-Publication Data

Benton, Jeffrey C., 1945–
Respectable and disreputable : leisure time in antebellum Montgomery, Alabama / Jeffrey C. Benton.

p. cm.

Includes bibliographical references and index.

ISBN 978-1-60306-229-9 (hardcover)
ISBN 978-1-60306-325-8 (ebook)

1. Montgomery (Ala.)—Social life and customs—19th century. 2. Leisure—Alabama—Montgomery—History—19th century. I. Title.
F334.M75B46 2012
976.1'47—dc23

2012037637

Design by Randall Williams
Printed in the United States of America

Sources of Illustrations

All images reproduced in this book are used with the permission of and through the courtesy of the Alabama Department of Archives and History, Montgomery, Alabama.

To Mary Ann Neeley, Montgomery's Historian

She approaches Montgomery, past and present, with the objectivity of a scholar and with the subjectivity of one in love with her city.

Contents

Acknowledgments / ix

Introduction / 3

1 Everyday Pastimes / 15

2 Seasonal Amusements and Diversions / 45

3 Commercial Entertainment / 65

Conclusion / 98

Notes / 102

Bibliography / 118

Index / 125

Acknowledgments

Almost all books are the result of a collaborative effort. Certainly this one is. I wish to thank the staffs of Auburn University's Ralph Brown Draughon Library and the Alabama Department of Archives and History. I am especially grateful to Meredith McLemore, Alabama Department of Archives and History, and to James Fuller, Montgomery County Historical Society, for making illustrations available.

I am also indebted to Mary Ann Neeley, longtime director of the Landmarks Foundation, who so graciously shares her knowledge of Montgomery—which is prodigious. Karen Heydon Benton, my wife, was instrumental in making suggestions on the text. The editorial work of NewSouth Books, was, of course, critical.

Without the dedication of Randall Williams of NewSouth Books, who has devoted his professional life to helping Montgomerians make their city a better place, this book would not be available for the general public.

Respectable and Disreputable

Portrait photograph of Louis Trezevant Wigfall (1816–74), probably taken in Montgomery in April 1861.

Introduction

William Howard Russell, a special correspondent for the London *Times*, related a conversation he had with Confederate Senator Louis T. Wigfall in Montgomery, Alabama, the Confederacy's provisional capital, in May 1861:

> We are a peculiar people, sir! You don't understand us, and you can't understand us, because we are known to you only by Northern writers and Northern papers, who know nothing of us themselves, or misrepresent what they do know. We are an agricultural people; we are a primitive but a civilized people. We have no cities—we don't want them. We have no literature—we don't need any yet. We have no press—we are glad of it. We do not require a press because we go out and discuss all public questions from the stump with our people . . . We want no manufactures: we desire no trading, no mechanical or manufacturing classes. As long as we have our rice, our sugar, our tobacco, and our cotton, we can command wealth to purchase all we want from those nations with which we are in amity, and to lay up money besides.[1]

Less confident men than Senator Wigfall might have paused to consider their immediate surroundings before proclaiming the existence of one distinctive South, a land of rural folk and rough-hewn culture. Montgomery was, after all, a city with several bookstores, newspapers, and a fine new theater. If Montgomery's cultural opportunities did not rival those available in New York, London or Paris, the city nonetheless had a cultural life that linked it to the urban centers in the North and Europe. Of course, Wigfall was exaggerating; he was known for hyperbole. The senator clearly left much unmentioned or unexplored in his remarks emphasizing Southern distinctiveness.

Of course it is human nature to emphasize differences and minimize similarities. There is no question that the antebellum South and North differed in significant ways, especially economically and in regards to slavery and all that that institution entailed. There were, however, powerful similarities, such as in basic human nature and in a shared religion, albeit with regional twists. This book questions the validity of a separate Southern cultural identity by considering the leisure activities of antebellum Montgomery, one aspect of the city's cultural life. How, for example, did the people of Montgomery differ from or resemble other Americans? Was Montgomery more like or unlike small cities in the North?

Leisure activities reveal social values, because those activities are freely chosen by individuals. Societies or individuals must invent ideals for how leisure time should be used. Because of increased leisure time, antebellum Americans were forced to question whether non-work time should be spent actively or passively, for entertainment and fun, or for education and profit—self-improvement, self-development, and self-expression. Should leisure be used as an opportunity for selfish conspicuous consumption or an opportunity for selfless service? Americans both North and South confronted these questions.

Discretionary income and time free from work—realities for increasing numbers of Americans during the antebellum period—made leisure activities possible. But what antebellum Americans did with their free time depended on individual and social values and on other factors: length and distribution of free time, leisure opportunities and frequency of those opportunities, demographics, class, education, taste, and community wealth and wealth distribution. A sketch of Montgomery's economy, population, and religion is required to understand the city's everyday pastimes, seasonal recreation, commercial entertainment, and intellectual pursuits, as well as the meanings of those activities.[2]

MONTGOMERY WAS FORMED in 1819 from New Philadelphia and East Alabama, two villages founded by land speculators who hoped to entice those moving west on the Federal Road to settle in Montgomery. In addition to the Federal Road—a great east-west artery of the early antebellum period—the

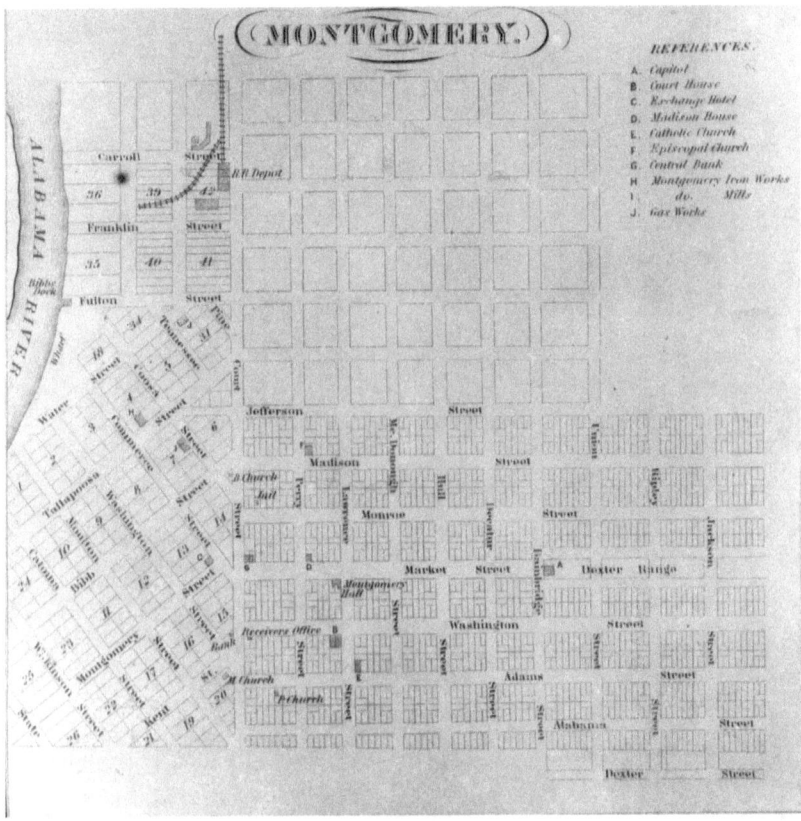

This early street map of Montgomery shows the north-south, east-west grid of New Philadelphia and the diagonal northwest-southeast, northeast-southwest grid of East Alabama Town.

town depended on the Alabama River and its partially navigable headwaters. Throughout the antebellum period, river traffic was the most important form of transportation to the city's economy. In the earliest years, flatboats and keelboats served the town on an irregular basis, but beginning in 1821 steamboats connected Montgomery with Mobile on regular schedules. Steamboat transportation reigned supreme because it carried the region's cotton to Mobile. Because Montgomery was at the upper reaches of the navigable river, its commercial influence extended over a larger radius than would have been the case if steamboats could have penetrated further north

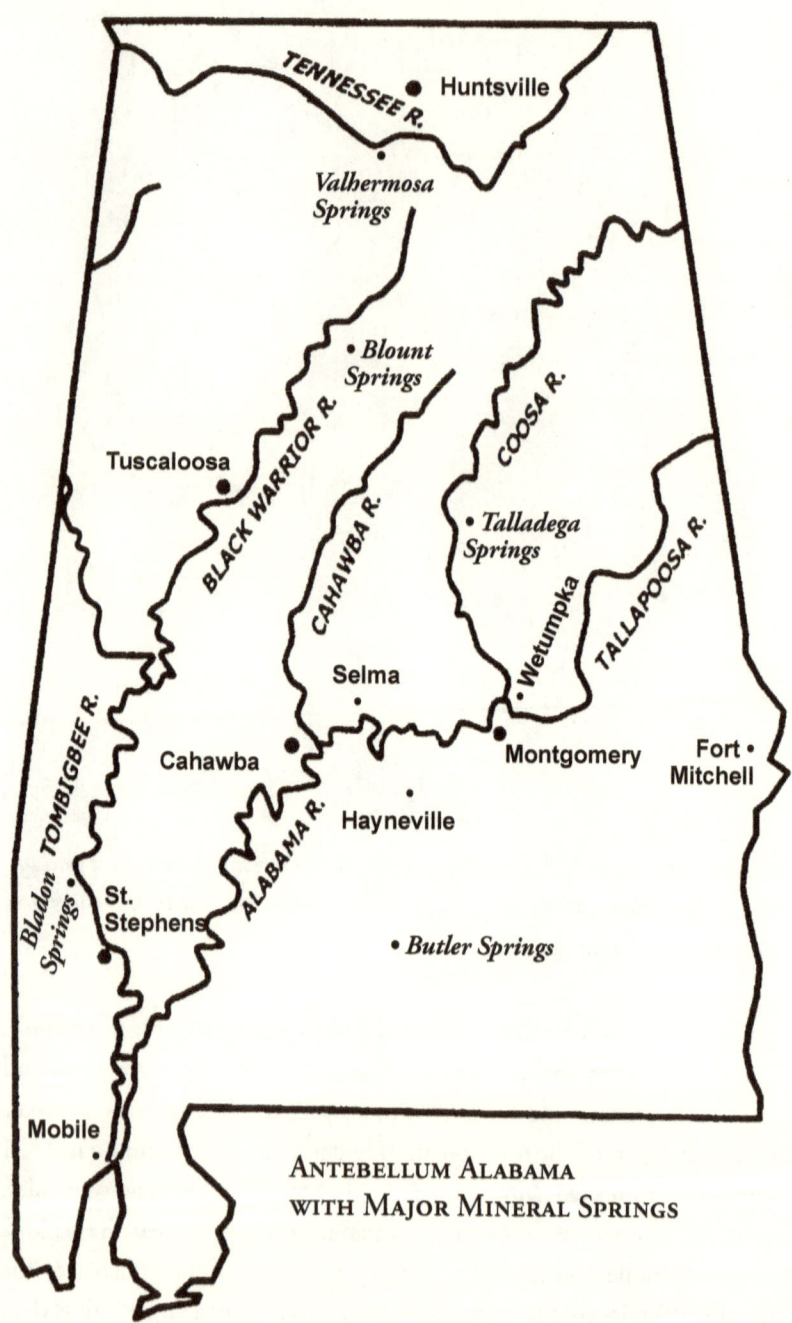

ANTEBELLUM ALABAMA WITH MAJOR MINERAL SPRINGS

into the state. Montgomery became even more of a transportation center as north and south plank roads and several railroads were developed in the 1840s. The railroad connection to Atlanta and the East was completed in 1851.[3] Being a transportation center positively affected not only the town's economy, but also ensured that Montgomerians and those in the surrounding hinterland had the opportunity to attend commercial performances given by troupes of entertainers traveling to and from Mobile and New Orleans.

The city's economy was overwhelmingly, but not exclusively, dependent on cotton. Retail and wholesale merchants, bankers, cotton factors, brokers and commission merchants served the cotton growers. However, the city also served as a government center and, to a small degree at the end of the antebellum period, as a manufacturing center. From 1822 Montgomery was the county seat, and from 1846 it was the state capital. Although Prattville, a few miles to the northwest, was antebellum Alabama's manufacturing center, by 1860 Montgomery had a foundry and an iron works, machine manufacturing shops, two tanneries, two furniture factories, a flouring mill, a hat-making factory, and a textile mill. The 1860 census listed the value of all Montgomery County manufactures as $293,850. The county also produced wool and a wide variety of foodstuffs: beef, pork, mutton, corn, wheat, rye, barley, peas, beans, Irish and sweet potatoes, rice, garden produce, fruit, milk, butter, cheese, honey, molasses, and wine.[4] Neither a military garrison nor an institution of higher learning directly influenced the economy—or values—of antebellum Montgomery. The city, a government and commercial center for an agricultural hinterland, was certainly wealthy enough to sustain a variety of public and private leisure activities. But as the economy basically depended on cotton, depressed prices could adversely affect commercial entertainment. Furthermore, wealth distribution and other demographic factors also affected leisure activities, especially as they influenced audience potential.

The size of Montgomery's potential audience and possibilities for financial success for entertainment promoters affected the city's leisure time opportunities. Montgomery's population climbed from 401 (239 whites and 162 blacks) in 1819 to 8,843 (4,341 whites and 4,502 blacks) in 1860.[5] Although slaves and women made up the majority of Montgomery's popu-

View of Montgomery from the north. Drawn by a special artist traveling with William Howard Russell, correspondent for The Times of London *and published in* Harper's Weekly, *June 1, 1861.*

lation, public leisure activities in Montgomery, as elsewhere in antebellum America, were largely reserved for adult white males. Slaves (paying half-price admissions) were allowed to attend some professional performances, but they certainly did not comprise their proportionate share of the audience. Their non-work time was restricted, as were their unsupervised activities. In antebellum America, potential participation in public leisure activities was diminished because women did not belong to the fraternal and learned societies and because few women attended commercial entertainment, such as the theater. Women's leisure was largely confined to their homes—to music, reading, and hospitality in a variety of forms. The relative low number of potential participants in leisure activities outside the home ensured that a variety of activities, especially commercial entertainment, could not be easily sustained. Population also influenced potential participation: Montgomery's population swelled in the fall after the cotton harvest or when the legislature was in session and declined during the heat of the long summers. The population, like that of so many other American cities, was large enough to attract commercial entertainers but often too small to sustain audiences sizeable enough to make commercial entertainment profitable.

The population of Montgomery's hinterland also contributed to potential participation in the city's leisure activities. Great wealth and large slaveholdings produced a leisure class, but such a class was not particularly large in antebellum Montgomery. No more than a third of the county's rural slaveholders were planters with plentiful leisure time. Most leisure activity participants from the county were small farmers, who comprised the majority of the rural white population. But even the small slaveholder was prosperous and could attend commercial entertainment. The population of the two counties just north of Montgomery, especially of the two nearby towns of Wetumpka and Prattville, also contributed participants to leisure activities in the city.

Wealth distribution influenced potential leisure activity participation. Slave ownership indicates overall wealth and its distribution. Slaves constituted 40 percent of the population in 1819, approximately half the population in 1840, and just over half in 1860. In 1840, 85 percent or 181 of the city's heads of households held slaves, the median number being four. As the number of whites engaged in manufacturing and other less remunerative work increased, wealth distribution based on slave ownership had changed significantly. By 1860, only 47 percent or 432 heads of households held slaves, and the median number held had decreased to just below four. In 1840 no family head owned more than thirty slaves, but by 1860 thirty heads of household did.[6]

Socioeconomic status played a role in the development of leisure activities in antebellum Montgomery. It did not, however, have the impact that it had in the North from the 1830s or would have nationally in the latter half of the century when elite and popular culture divided along class lines. In much of the United States, class in the broad sense—mutually exclusive groups based on family, wealth, occupation, education level and school, religious denomination, spatial separation, and taste—was just solidifying in the decade before the Civil War. Wealth, more than any other factor, determined social status, especially in the more recently settled areas. Wealth allowed its possessors to engage in conspicuous consumption, but fine clothing, houses, and horses and carriages could not magically transform the wealthy into an authentic "aristocracy" overnight. By the end of the period, mobility into the elite had decreased, as wealthy families intermarried and formed more of a closed group. How families acquired wealth mattered little; many of the greatest landowners in the county also invested in business and were included among the incorporators of Montgomery's railroads, wharf and steamboat companies, insurance companies, hotels, gas light company, water works, race course association, and manufacturing companies.[7]

The 1860 manuscript census identified twenty-eight planters and six "gentlemen" living in the city; three manufacturer/industrialists and approximately seventy-five large merchants were also identified. These men and their families, and planting families living in close proximity to the city, comprised the elite. As planters directly and indirectly dominated Montgomery's economy, urban commercial groups lacked economic independence, an essential characteristic of the middle class. In this book, middling classes (a contemporary term for those between the elite and those engaged in manual labor) refers to Montgomery's approximately one hundred professionals, an additional hundred medium and small merchants, and two hundred clerks and bookkeepers. Many of the latter group were beginning their careers as businessmen. An additional two hundred mechanics, or artisans, occupied an even more ambiguous position than the clerks. Their place in Southern society was complicated by slavery: although skilled, mechanics worked with their hands, work certainly not as respectable in a slave society as in a free one, where mechanics exhibited some middle-class characteristics. Except during economic downturns, members of the elite and the upper half of the middling classes had ample leisure time and the financial wherewithal to attend commercial entertainment. Clerks, bookkeepers, and mechanics could afford the time and admission to attend occasionally, especially if they were unmarried. On the other hand, a portion of the white population of both city and hinterland was so poor that its leisure time and participation in commercial entertainment were very limited. The daily wages of servants and common laborers with families only allowed for infrequent attendance at commercial entertainment. In 1860 this group numbered approximately 140; their numbers probably increased as a percentage of the white population during the period.[8]

Montgomery's elite—in 1860, approximately a hundred planters and large merchants and their families—contributed to the success of various leisure activities, despite their small numbers and their absence from the city for long periods during the year. Professionals, especially lawyers, disproportionately provided leadership for many leisure activities, and the remainder of the middling classes furnished the numbers that made those activities succeed or fail. Their involvement may represent a middle class struggling to establish itself.

Place of origin played a minor role in determining participation in leisure activities. In the early years, settlers dubbed New Philadelphia "Yankee Town" because of the disproportionate number of Northerners in its population. Northerners figured prominently in voluntary societies having intellectual and practical objectives. New Englanders may have tended to oppose the theater, horse racing, and other commercial entertainment more than Southerners, but they were not alone in their opposition. During the 1850s the portion of Northern-born family heads declined from a fifth to a tenth of Montgomery family heads. Their influence, however, remained significant in the city's commercial and civil life.

While the percentage of Northern-born family heads decreased and that of Southern-born family heads remained stable, the percentage of foreign-born Montgomerians increased. During the 1850s, foreign-born heads of families rose from a fifth to a quarter. Of these household heads, forty-five in 1850 and 113 in 1860 did not speak English as their native language; these represented 8 percent and 12 percent of the total heads of household. Although immigrants did not significantly influence the city's leisure activities, they did organize several societies: the French Benevolent Society in 1830, Chevra Mevacher Cholim in 1846, and a German Odd Fellows Lodge in 1854—membership in these societies was not restricted to the foreign born.[9]

Religion also helped shape the nature of and participation in leisure activities. Throughout the antebellum period, most Protestant denominations disapproved of the theater and, to a lesser degree, other commercial entertainment. Many also disapproved of dancing, frowned on intemperate drinking, and, later, opposed drinking altogether. But the Northeast, not the Southeast, was more strongly affected by the great religious revivals of the period. Proscriptions against the theater and horse racing, for example, were strongest and most successful in New England. Religion exerted relatively little influence in early Montgomery. Infrequent services were held in private houses, taverns, or the courthouse. Even when a nondenominational church building went up in the early 1820s, religion failed to prosper and preaching was infrequent.[10]

Montgomery's first revival coincided with the climax of the Second Great Awakening, the series of revivals most often associated with the Northeast.[11] In November 1831, Eliza Goddard Whitman Pickett, who was connected with several of Montgomery's most prominent families, wrote to her sister in Maine that the theater and the newly dedicated Presbyterian Church were the finest buildings in Montgomery, and that

> There has been a great revival of religion in this town . . . no amusements whatever, even our splendid theatre . . . a talk has been to make it a Methodist church—I think they will succeed in obtaining it for that purpose as the church they now ocupy is getting old and the goats have mostly taken posession of it.[12]

Religious facilities improved markedly between 1831 and 1837, as Presbyterians, Baptists, Methodist Protestants, Universalists, Roman Catholics, Methodist Episcopals, and Episcopalians constructed church buildings. Revivals in 1839 and 1845 added members to the original congregations, but by the close of the antebellum period only the Baptists and Methodists had founded second churches, and these were very small. Although church membership climbed throughout the period, it comprised an insignificant part of Montgomery's population, as it did nationally, where less than a fifth of the population was churched by 1850. However, membership, which was strictly controlled, is not an accurate gauge of the influence of religion, because considerably more people attended services than were members.

Membership in Montgomery's Protestant churches was not rigidly stratified by socioeconomic status. As elsewhere in the United States, Methodists and Baptists had become respectable by mid-century. Some members of Montgomery's wealthiest and most influential families belonged to the Baptist and Methodist churches, although the Presbyterian and Episcopal churches appear to have attracted more of the elite. Overall, membership in the city's Protestant churches seems to have been fluid; individuals occasionally changed denominations, and members of nuclear families were found in more than one denomination.[13]

Religious strictures sometimes limited leisure activities. Montgomery Presbyterians, for example, expelled members for intemperance and drunkenness, profane language, attending balls, and dancing.[14] In 1860 the wife of an Alabama Presbyterian minister wrote in her diary:

> No *evangelical church* in Christendom *sanctions* dancing any more than attending theatres—horse races—or chicken fighting—card playing or lotteries—wine drinking or dissipation in any shape. And so far as individual members transgress—in these respects they weaken their moral sense of rectitude, lower their standard of piety and when the fact becomes *notorious*—brings a scandal upon the church of Christ, a blemish upon their own good name.[15]

Even some Episcopal ministers disapproved of participating in ordinary entertainment. The Right Reverend Doctor Nicholas Hamner Cobbs, first Episcopal Bishop of Alabama (1844–61) and rector of Montgomery's Episcopal church (1852–61), "very persistently and aggressively . . . contend[ed] against theatre-going and ball-room dancing, and, while he did not censoriously judge those whose profession was to teach dancing, he distinctly affirmed that he would not confirm a dancing-master."[16]

The weather also influenced potential audiences. During hot summers, when large numbers of people could not comfortably assemble indoors, traveling troupes often disbanded. Many wealthier Montgomerians left the city. Other weather conditions—particularly heavy rains that made the roads impassable and drought that slowed river traffic—also affected entertainment, as did outbreaks of smallpox and yellow fever, and economic booms and depressions.[17]

THE DEVELOPMENT OF Montgomery's leisure activities, especially those of the middling classes, paralleled development elsewhere in antebellum America. Although a strong middle class had not developed in Montgomery by the end of the antebellum period, Montgomerians had to one degree or another experimented with those institutions, especially voluntary associations, that were so closely associated with middle class formation in the North. Montgomerians faced the same challenges in defining appropriate uses of leisure time; with some notable exceptions, such as competitive team sports and women's voluntary associations, they embraced the same activities as other Americans. Several trends characterize the development of leisure activities during the period. A relatively common culture became increasingly stratified and diverse. Participatory activities became relatively less important, as the variety and frequency of spectator activities increased and as some agendas of the voluntary associations were passed to political parties. Local control, consequently, was slowly lost to regional and national commercial entertainment entrepreneurs. How Montgomery followed these national trends illustrates how homogenized one aspect of American culture had become by the advent of the Civil War. Of course, culture in its broadest connotations displayed major regional differences, but a part of culture—leisure activities—discloses that antebellum Americans had a great deal in common.

1

Everyday Pastimes

The most common leisure activity in antebellum America was visiting with family, friends and acquaintances. People ate, drank, gossiped, told stories, read aloud, and played games and music. In general, these activities centered on the home and involved men and women of all classes. Men, however, dominated almost all public leisure activities. Some activities, such as public drinking, gambling and sporting were exclusively reserved for men. These pastimes, often associated with the free-wheeling individuality of the newly settled towns, also existed in larger towns and cities in longer-settled areas of the country.

The changing nature of work shaped male leisure patterns. During the antebellum period, America's middling classes acquired leisure time, a luxury previously reserved for the elite. Increasing numbers of urban white men worked away from their places of residence. Fewer were self-employed; more worked for wages. The work day, which had included nearly all waking hours, shortened, but work itself intensified. The old norm of the "shop-house," in which master and helpers lived and worked together, fostered a personal relationship among the workers whose long hours of low-intensity activity were frequently interspersed with short breaks. Many workers talked as they worked, and many drank during breaks, but with and under the supervision of the master. As this system broke down, masters and workers traded many short periods of non-work for longer, but less frequent periods of leisure. Unlike the elite, the middling classes had few traditional pastimes to fill newly acquired, concentrated leisure time. Not until after the Civil War were numerous leisure activities available for the middling classes.

At first, the middling classes adopted formerly elite leisure activities, such as thoroughbred horse racing, the theater and gambling. Workers began to drink more, but no longer with or under their masters' supervision. The elite

Ambrotype of two unidentified young women with a guitar. Because of their restrictive clothing, women tended to play instruments that did not require them to lift their arms above mid-chest.

and especially the emerging middle class came to see the tendency towards unrestrained leisure activities—especially heavy drinking and gambling—as a social control problem and as a threat to the work ethic and family life.

In communities throughout the United States, both the rougher male pastimes and the efforts to control them—instilling social order and establishing a sense of community—influenced the use of leisure time. Although Southern religious revivals may not have elicited the degree of social reform that the Second Great Awakening did in the North, Montgomery's city council and churches tried to restrict entertainment and enforce strict observation of the Sabbath. Throughout the antebellum period Americans attempted to distinguish between appropriate and inappropriate leisure time activities. Many men used their leisure time for activities other than, or in addition to, gambling, drinking and sporting.[1]

Gambling, Drinking, and Sporting

Like other American towns and cities, Montgomery had a raw edge, which lingered even after the first years of settlement. Gambling, excessive drinking, prostitution and brawling—prevalent throughout the country—could be denied, avoided, overlooked or hidden in larger cities, but they dominated many smaller towns in newly settled areas. Albert James Pickett, one of Alabama's earliest historians, personally observed Montgomery's development from its founding.

> Cocks were fought in the public square by the most prominent men in the place. Murder often occurred and fighting was so common that it scarcely attracted attention. I do state, with a knowledge of the facts, that it was once the most dissipated, wicked place I ever saw, but I am happy to state, that it is now [1852] a highly refined, moral and religious community.[2]

Efforts to tame Montgomery's rough aspects and to control what were believed by some to be inappropriate leisure activities on the Sabbath preceded the revivals of 1831, 1839 and 1845. In conformity with a national movement to observe the Sabbath strictly, the town council passed Montgomery's first Sabbath observation ordinance in January 1820:

> . . . no worldly business or employment or ordinary, or servile work (works of necessity or charity excepted) no gaming fiddling or other musick for the sake of merriment nor any kind of play, sports, pastimes or diversions shall be done performed or practiced by any person or persons within the limits of Said Town on the first day of the week commonly called The Sabbath, and every person of the age of fifteen years or upwards offending in the premises shall for every such offence forfeit and pay the sum of one dollar.[3]

Subsequently the council frequently addressed violations of Sabbath ordinances and tried to strengthen the resolve of the watch, patrols and police to enforce them. Although no new Sabbath observation ordinances were recorded after 1849, as late as July 1860 the city council maintained that it would enforce prohibitions on the sale of liquor and cigars on Sundays. Still, Montgomery's Sabbath ordinances did not restrict leisure activities as they were restricted in New England, nor do they seem to have been strictly enforced. Similar ordinances elsewhere also proved unenforceable, and may have merely served to separate the respectable and disreputable.[4]

Antebellum Americans bet on cock fights, boxing matches, billiards, and foot, horse and boat races. What in England had been largely a pastime for the elite was open to all in nineteenth century America. Professional gambling in saloons, in specialized gaming houses and on steamboats, however, became a problem in the 1830s. Local elites, who had dominated gambling, lost control to professionals and came to see gambling, especially when it involved professionals and the lower strata of society, as a social control problem. Although professional gambling knew no regional boundaries, it was commonly associated with the West, where men gambled openly and enthusiastically. Gambling also reflected the unrestrained commercialism and get-rich-quick attitude of many Americans. In the South particularly, those with aristocratic aspirations or pretensions may have gambled to mimic the behavior of the English gentry.[5]

Many believed that government-sanctioned lotteries, which had been used

Primitive painting of Alexander Faim's Tavern with the first Montgomery capitol under construction in the background, c. 1847. This is the oldest known painting of Montgomery.

since colonial times to raise monies for public projects, fostered widespread gambling that the authorities could not easily control. Advertisements for domestic and foreign lotteries appeared frequently in Montgomery's newspapers. But as Montgomery sponsored few lotteries, revenues that could have been used for local improvements flowed out of the community. In 1821 the General Assembly granted several Montgomerians the right to hold a five thousand dollar lottery to raise money to build an academy. Five years later the state authorized a ten thousand dollar academy lottery; its two thousand tickets were to yield more than eight hundred prizes ranging from five dollars to a thousand dollars. Neither Montgomery school lottery materialized. In 1834 the state not only wanted to authorize local lotteries, but also to authorize sale of all lottery tickets. The five hundred dollar fine for selling unauthorized lottery tickets indicated the state's seriousness about controlling lotteries—as gambling and as revenue sources. In 1843 Montgomery required lottery ticket sellers to be licensed by the city. In the 1830s lotteries began to be forbidden, first in the North. By the end of the antebellum period every state had banned lotteries.[6] American society was turning away from this relatively benign form of gambling.

Lotteries were much easier to control than professional gambling. They served as voluntary tax mechanisms, and traditional betting merely redistributed wealth within a community, but professional gambling stripped local amateurs of their wealth. Professional gambling, as opposed to private non-commercial gambling, became a major social control problem in antebellum America that state and local authorities tried to regulate. Professional gambling had become such a problem in Montgomery by 1821 that a local newspaper called for controlling the dregs of society whom the editor believed were destroying the town's morals. In October 1825 and again in February 1853, elements of Montgomery's population applauded the presentation of Edward Moore's *The Gamester*, which portrayed a young man being led to ruin and death by uncontrolled gaming. At least one letter to the editor recommended the play as an antidote to the disease of gambling.[7]

States routinely legislated against public gaming. In general, Southern legislation targeted professional gamblers and the poor, ignoring the elite. In the North exhortations to work and save complemented legislation against public gaming. The state of Alabama passed several anti-gambling laws with substantial penalties. In 1821 the shell game was forbidden on penalty of three hours in the pillory and a five hundred to two thousand dollar fine for the holder of the game. Casual bettors, presumed to be victims, were not punished. In 1825 municipalities were forbidden to license gaming houses, although previously granted licenses were not repealed. The fine for betting in an unlicensed house ranged from twenty to five hundred dollars. More sophisticated games, such as roulette, faro, and rouge et noir, were proscribed in 1827. Holders of the games were fined one thousand dollars or three months in jail; players' fines ranged from ten to a hundred dollars. An 1834 statute required officers of the state bank and its branches to forswear gambling, and an 1836 statute prohibited adults from gambling with minors. In 1853 betting over billiards was punishable by a fine of at least one hundred dollars or imprisonment from three to six months. Nationally and locally anti-gambling laws were largely ineffective. Although the laws reflected the desire of civil and church authorities to determine appropriate leisure activity, they clashed with the chosen behavior of the population.[8]

Montgomery's council repeatedly tried to limit professional gambling and public drunkenness. Considering the frequent reorganizations of the night slave patrol, a mandatory duty of white males eighteen to forty-five, with the exception of members of the volunteer military units and fire companies, control appears to have been beyond the powers of the town's authorities. "The Gentry," a group of gamblers, essentially ran the town in the mid-1830s, intimidating those who opposed their disruptive gambling, drinking and brawling. John Thorington, Montgomery's intendant, or mayor, tried to establish civil authority in the first half of 1835. Ordinances against gambling, horse racing in the streets and discharging firearms inside the corporate limits failed, in part because Thorington and the town council could not compel the law enforcement officers to confront "The Gentry." Incensed because the gang threw his carriage into the Alabama River, Colonel Thorington led a group of several hundred citizens against the gamblers. He arrested the gang's ringleader, Captain Isaac Ticknor, who had himself been Montgomery's intendant in 1833. In early 1836, many of "The Gentry," under the command of Captain Ticknor, left Montgomery for Texas—only to be massacred at Goliad. Apparently fearing for their safety, Colonel Thorington and many of his family also left Montgomery that spring.

Montgomery had not seen the end of the lawlessness of the gamblers. Trouble erupted again in August 1837 with provocations, a shooting, a disembowelment with a bowie knife, a jailbreak and an ambush of the posse that was trying to apprehend Kenyon Mooney and his gang. Mooney, however, operated with impunity until late 1839, when he left the state. Because Montgomery's council had failed to deal effectively with the lawlessness of the gamblers, the 1837 legislative act establishing Montgomery as a city required that its elected officials swear to control gambling and the city's riotous elements. Montgomery's efforts against professional gambling corresponded to efforts—often vigilante—throughout the Old Southwest during the 1830s.

Newspaper advertisement for Hole in the Wall, Jr., which was a new watering hole on the ground floor of the newly opened Montgomery Theatre building. Montgomery Daily Advertiser, *13 November 1860.*

Gambling declined in the South because it was connected with criminals, not because it was considered a vice or because it was not genteel—gambling retained its aristocratic connotations. Nationally gambling, at least public gambling, was not considered respectable.[9]

Montgomery's 1835 anti-gambling ordinance included bowling and billiards, because they were used for gambling. The council subsequently amended the ordinance, allowing billiard saloons and nine pin alleys that were not used for gambling.[10] Billiards had wide appeal; Montgomery's elite played the game in private homes, in the city's finer hotels, or in

> . . . one of the most splendid BILLIARDS ROOMS in the Southern country . . . for the accommodation of all those who delight in this most euphoneous and healthful exercise . . . [for] the pleasure and taste of the most fastidious . . . where pleasure and leisure may be employed with a levity that distains all pursuit.[11]

Excessive drinking, although not considered to be as serious a social control problem as gambling, presented problems for all socioeconomic groups throughout Montgomery's entire antebellum period. On Christmas Day, 1834, Tyrone Power, the prominent Irish comedian, stopped in Montgomery for two hours before departing by steamboat for Mobile. His comments regarding the passengers, mostly planters, certainly applied to some residents of Montgomery:

> ... they were a rough but merry set of fellows, and many of them exceedingly intelligent; kinder or better disposed men I never met: for their own health's sake I could have desired to see the bar less prosperous; their visits to that quarter were over frequent; not that an instance of inebriety occurred on board, but the stimulant, together with the quantity of tobacco they use, must, I am sure, be ruinous to both health and enjoyment.[12]

In 1839 James Buckingham, a lecturer and retired member of Parliament, observed that excessive drinking was a cause of Mobile's degeneracy and immoral behavior.[13]

Americans consumed prodigious quantities of alcohol between 1790 and 1830, more than at any other time in the country's history. Early Montgomerians imported alcohol in great quantities. In May 1826, one merchant received seventy barrels of whiskey; another merchant advertised cognac, gin, port and Madeira, as well as whiskey. By the last decade of the period, the brandy, hock, burgundy, sherry and champagne drunk in private homes, hotels and restaurants posed few problems, but the swilling of whiskey and beer in saloons threatened public order. Most cases of drunk and disorderly conduct brought before the mayor's court occurred in saloons or brothels. Men of all socioeconomic groups frequented taverns in the early days; later hotels and restaurants catered to the wealthier drinkers. Although some saloons offered fine fare, cigars and liquors, most saloons became working men's clubs in which masculine comradeship, sociability and drinking rituals were expected, and rowdiness, gambling and prostitution were tolerated.[14]

Unlike government attempts to regulate professional gambling, control of excessive drinking and its consequences were generally confined to the mayor's court. However, local ordinances prohibited both slaves and free blacks from gambling and drinking. Although most slaves worked under the supervision of their masters, as white male workers had in traditional households and workshops, a sufficient number lived and worked separately from their masters; this situation concern the city's authorities. Ordinances forbade slaves to gamble, to assemble (except in very small numbers), and to drink, except on the premises and with the permission of their masters. Montgomery's council tried various other restrictions: separation of slaves and free blacks, passes, evening curfew, Sabbath observation and, especially, retail liquor regulations. Offenders were subject to flogging or fines. Ordinances required slaves to have their masters' written permission to purchase liquor and restricted the quantities that merchants could sell to slaves. Retail liquor licensees took oaths to uphold the ordinances. The council frequently ordered the watch, patrols and police to enforce the ordinances rigorously. But these unrelenting efforts failed to control blacks' pastimes, as did efforts to prohibit whites from violating the Sabbath and gambling publicly. The ordinances reflected the values and concerns of Montgomery's officials and the more affluent members of the middling classes. But neither slaves, free blacks, nor probably the white masses were interested in social control. Both the police and the citizenry, as represented in the patrols, were unwilling to enforce Montgomery's ordinances consistently.[15]

Baptist, Methodist and Presbyterian churches viewed excessive drinking—later, drinking at all—as a serious moral problem. Montgomerians founded their first Temperance Society in 1832, just six years after the American Temperance Society was founded in Boston. This was followed by the Temperance Society of Montgomery County in 1841, which became the Washingtonian Society in 1843. The first Washingtonian Society, founded in Baltimore in 1840, advocated abstinence, not temperance. Washingtonian efforts to reform already intemperate drinkers conflicted with Temperance Society efforts to keep temperate drinkers from becoming excessive drinkers.

Furthermore, as mechanics, or artisans, dominated the ranks of the Washingtonians, socioeconomic differences between the two movements fueled the conflict. These differences did not come to a head in Montgomery, because the Washingtonians did not operate autonomously, but in conjunction with the temperance societies, and because prominent citizens led both Washingtonian and temperance societies. Both groups held public demonstrations and occasionally sponsored out-of-town speakers. Father Theobold Matthew, the Irish "Apostle of Temperance," who had administered the temperance pledge to half the population of Ireland and to half a million Americans during his twenty-eight month tour, administered the pledge to hundreds of Montgomerians in February 1850. Montgomery's Sons of Temperance, organized in 1847, five years after the national fraternal order was founded, appealed to those in the middling classes who chose to use their leisure time constructively. Sons of Temperance took pledges of abstinence in simple initiation ceremonies, which the founders of the order believed would help sustain interest in the temperance movement. The Sons of Temperance, dominated by Baptists and the poor, became the most important temperance society in Alabama. In the North, where teetotalism had become associated with middle-class respectability, the majority of states had prohibited alcohol by mid-century. However, in a hard-fought campaign in 1855, Alabama's Sons of Temperance failed to have an anti-drinking agenda adopted as state law. Yet the fraternity remained active throughout the remainder of the antebellum period. Two temperance newspapers were published in Montgomery for short times: the *Orion*, later *Sons of Temperance*, in 1848–49 and the *Southern Times* in 1855–56.[16]

Unlike gambling and drinking, neither the authorities nor the churches saw prostitution as a social control problem. During the nineteenth century, common law considered prostitution to be a kind of vagrancy, not a criminal offense. Antebellum Alabama laws did not prohibit prostitution directly; however, as elsewhere, laws existed against adultery. Some localities prohibited keeping houses of prostitution. Yet, in many places, raucous brothels, as well as decorous "parlor houses" for discriminating customers, went unregulated. Sporadic moral reform efforts made little headway against prostitution, and physicians and the police mostly attempted to regulate, rather than abolish, the trade. Slavery added its own twist to the national toleration of prostitution: it made prostitution unnecessary for many in the slaveowning class that could, if they chose, resort to slave concubinage rather than patronize prostitutes. During the summers, wealthy Montgomerians could take advantage of gambling, drinking and sporting in resort establishments. Saratoga, New York, one of the country's finest resorts, was noted for all three activities.[17]

Montgomery's experience with prostitution seems to have mirrored that of the country. In February 1838, the city council prohibited the keeping of brothels within the city limits—they had previously been legal. Each person living in such an establishment could be fined up to fifty dollars. An April 1842 ordinance established a thirty to fifty dollar fine for property owners who rented their premises for the purposes of prostitution. Laws, of course, did not end prostitution.[18] Brothels may have moved just outside the corporation limits to Bogue Homme, a separate community on the South Plank Road, where "homage [was paid] to Mars, Apollo and Baccus."[19] A humorous account of the proceedings of the mayor's court in March 1860 indicates the lax attitude towards prostitution:

> A half dozen *nymphs du pave* were before the Mayor yesterday—some as witnesses, others as principals in a case of disorderly conduct. Modesty, one of the attributes of female character, was at a considerable discount. It appears that a couple of the abandoned creatures had got into a quarrel about their respective "friends"—neither of whom we thought an Adonis in personal appearance—and talked in such a loud and angry tone—used so little discretion in the choice of words—as to both shock and disturb their neighbors, who made the complaint. Both were fined $10 and costs.[20]

The disorderly conduct and violence associated with the brothels concerned the authorities more than prostitution did. One newspaper editor, bemused by the goings-on in the brothels, criticized the "ungallant act of a young man in drawing an axe on, and threatening to kill, a frail fair one, who had displeased him."[21] Two weeks later the editor reported another altercation in the brothels in which a man who "perpetually wears a black eye as an emblem of his belligerent disposition" accused a female neighbor in "a red hot lava-tide of choice Billingsgate" of stealing a hen and of keeping a "house of ill-fame." The "widow" was given the "usual fine of $30."[22] In mid-April 1860 another prostitute was assaulted by "a *couple* of graceless scamps who maltreated her in a shameful manner . . ." The editor moralized:

> The act of assaulting a female, we believe, is classed amongst the most cowardly ever committed by a man. Occasionally, however, some gay lothario, with Don Quixote-like courage, violates this well established principle of propriety, and forfeits his claim to manliness by assaulting

and beating a frail piece of femininity.²³

Prostitution differed from public gambling or excessive drinking in that it was not believed to threaten social order; in a perverse way, it and slave concubinage were believed to help keep unmarried women inviolate and married ones chaste, while allowing men to be promiscuous.

Efforts to control these male pastimes focused on the behavior of those deemed to threaten public order, the lower strata of society and blacks, not on private gambling among gentlemen, social drinking or slave concubinage. Male pastimes were not, of course, confined to gambling, drinking and sporting. Hunting and fishing for sport had a broad appeal, whereas participation in literary societies and fraternal associations was more narrowly focused.

Hunting

Southern men of all socioeconomic groups fished and hunted, either to supplement their diets or as a leisure activity. Although hunting in America did not have the aristocratic associations that it carried in Europe, Daniel R. Hundley, an Alabama gentleman writing about Southern social classes at the end of the antebellum period, identified angling and sport hunting as of particular importance to the gentleman-planter. The South's low population density and overwhelmingly rural nature ensured that many men of the middling classes also had easy access to sport hunting. In Montgomery the planter and city elite were almost synonymous, and the more affluent members of the middling classes were closely allied with the planting elite. Sport hunting in the Northeast, however, differed. By mid-century hunting had also become a sport of the urban elite, but those sportsmen had to rely on clubs for access to hunting. Consequently, hunting was much more confined to the elite than it was in more rural areas of the country.²⁴

In the United States specialized sporting equipment became widely available from the 1830s. Several Montgomery outfitters, such as William Wright's Huntsman's and Fisherman's Emporium, sold sportsmen's clothing, guns, game bags, shot pouches and belts, and angling equipment, including assorted fishing lines.²⁵ Fine specialized equipment helped establish hunting and fishing as sports, rather than as practical activities.

The legal hunting season, which began in mid-September and continued through the end of the year, allowed for a wide variety of hunting methods, many of which required significant resources such as drovers, horses, hunting dogs, and large tracts of land. Men usually hunted deer, fox and boar from horseback, but some hunted deer by canoe at night, petrifying the deer with lantern light. Packs of dogs also drove deer to hunters in stationary positions; older gentlemen particularly enjoyed this still-hunting. Turkeys were hunted from blinds or were flushed from the underbrush by dogs. Hunters also used dogs to tree opossums and to corner rabbits. Hunters attracted birds by burning pine knots and then whipped them down with long switches.[26]

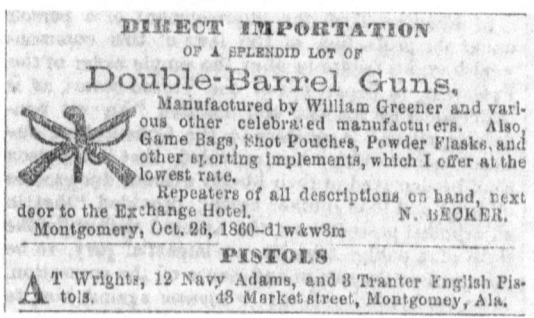

Newspaper advertisement for imported double-barrel guns, etc., Montgomery Weekly Advertiser, *December 26, 1860.*

The marksmanship skills of men and boys of the Alabama Black Belt astonished an English visitor:

> Self-defense, and the natural craving for excitement, compel him to be a hunter, and it is the appropriate occupation of a new, grand, luxuriant, wild country like this, and one which seems natural to man, to judge from the eagerness and zest with which every one engages in it when he has the opportunity. The long rifle is familiar to every hand; skill in the use of it is the highest accomplishment which a southern gentleman glories in; even children acquire an astonishing expertness in handling this deadly weapon at a very early age.[27]

Feats of marksmanship—"driving the nail," "threading the needle,"

"Deer-shooting by night," from a drawing by Philip Henry Gosse, Letters from Alabama, (U.S.): Chiefly Relating to Natural History, *London: Morgan and Chase, 1859. Gosse made the drawing in 1838 when he served as a schoolmaster in Dallas County.*

"snuffing the candle," and "barking off" squirrels—were actually commonplace. In the 1830s, John James Audubon observed "barking off," or killing a squirrel, not with the bullet, but with a piece of bark knocked off the tree by a bullet hitting just below the squirrel. Such skills, of course, came from frequent practice. Country folk had more opportunity to shoot, but many Montgomerians also hunted and challenged one another in shooting matches. Such events could take on social aspects pitting teams of gentlemen against one another. A social event that involved the ladies, such as a ball, might follow a shooting match or hunt.[28]

In the second quarter of the nineteenth century, fishing and hunting

Cup awarded to William Lowndes Yancey for marksmanship in May 1856. An accompanying note by Yancey's son states: "My father was an honorary member of the Montgomery True Blues, one of the oldest volunteer military companies in Alabama. In May 1856, encamped at Berumer's Garden upon the Alabama River bluff south of Montgomery, he won this cup as the best marksman of the order. Sept 23rd, 1903." Born in Georgia, Yancey spent his youth in Troy, New York. In 1837, after marrying a wealthy slave owner, he changed his antislavery views and moved to Alabama. He became an ardent Fire-Eater and arch-secessionist.

lost their practical aspects as they were transformed into sports. Angling, which was also enjoyed by women, and sport hunting were recognized as appropriate leisure activities for the elite of the great Northeastern cities and for a broader spectrum of the population in the smaller cities and towns of antebellum America. Large estates, significant tracts of unimproved land, and slaves to assist with hunts contributed to making many of the methods of sport hunting followed in the South different from those followed elsewhere. Angling and sport hunting were connected with the country's frontier heritage, and city people fished and hunted because they were attracted to rural pastimes. Some held to the practices of their rural backgrounds; others were attracted to a rural ideal to counter the realities of urban growth; and, especially among the elite, field sports were associated with aristocratic European behavior. Although followed by those who lived in cities, neither angling nor sport hunting represented leisure activities that were widely held to be appropriate for urban Americans.

Voluntary Associations

Voluntary associations grew in number, membership and importance throughout the nineteenth century. Closely associated with the growing and developing urban middle class, they fulfilled individual, social and civic needs, and were widely accepted as a legitimate use of leisure time—as opposed to gambling, drinking and sporting and to commercial entertainment that were widely condemned, especially by the evangelical churches.

White male Montgomerians created a variety of voluntary religious, charitable, learned, literary, political, theatrical, musical, social, fraternal and military associations. Many were short-lived or of limited appeal; all had social implications. Some were socially exclusive, such as the Bachelor's Club and the Benedict Club, which existed purely for pleasure, unlike those societies that professed noble purposes. Church authorities approved of many of these associations, especially the learned and literary societies, because they offered a profitable use of leisure by providing means for adult self-improvement. Although cities in the North had societies for women, Montgomery's voluntary associations catered to men, mainly men of substance, or at least of promise.[29]

The Franklin Society, the first such group in Montgomery, was founded in February 1821 "to encourage a literary taste and to improve the members in debating important issues."[30] During the first half of the century, Franklin literary and debating societies spread throughout the United States; most large towns had at least one such society whose purpose was the moral, social, mental and economic self-improvement of the young male members. In a time of great geographic mobility, such societies also substituted for the emotional support of families. Montgomery's Franklin Society addressed a variety of cultural, economic and political topics between 1823 and 1829: the ways and means to build a church, federal interference with Creek Indian affairs, whether or not the town should build a theater, and banking—all issues of importance in Montgomery.[31] The Franklin Society, like others that followed, such as the Young Men's Debating Society, flourished and then floundered.

The Lyceum Association and affiliated Library Association were founded in early 1843 by Enoch L. Childs, an 1840 graduate of Yale College and the first principal of the Montgomery Academy; the Reverend Andrew A. Lipscomb, a native of Virginia, nationally noted scholar and orator, and first minister of Montgomery's Methodist Protestant Church; and Colonel Francis

Bugbee, a Northerner, lawyer, state legislator, and trustee of the University of Alabama from 1836 to 1871.[32] The vision of these men for the future of the city represented antebellum Montgomery's most progressive element.

The American Lyceum movement, which may have encouraged reading more than any other antebellum institution, began in Massachusetts in late 1826, about two years after the movement began in London. The movement flourished in New England because a thriving middle-class culture, supported by the elite, was best developed in that region.[33] The Lyceum movement's objectives were:

> to procure for youths an economical and practical education, and to diffuse rational and useful information through the community generally . . . [and] to apply the sciences and various branches of education to the domestic and useful arts, and to all the common purposes of life.[34]

Lyceum education was based on an integrated and organized system of lectures that were supplemented by a library of technical books. The lectures were intended to offer knowledge of practical, scientific subjects such as mechanics, hydrostatics, pneumatics, chemistry, botany and mineralogy. Politics and religion were expressly excluded.[35]

Montgomery's Lyceum, however, did not strictly follow the basic guidelines regarding lecture subject matter. In March 1843 the Reverend Lipscomb delivered the Montgomery Lyceum's first lecture, "American Mind." Local notables gave free lectures weekly. Henry Hilliard, sometimes professor, lawyer, editor, diplomat, and Methodist minister, spoke on "Our Country and its Relations with the World." Schoolmaster Enoch Childs, however, adhered to the intentions of the Lyceum movement by presenting a series of lectures on chemistry, which he preceded with a lecture entitled "Study of the Natural Sciences." The 1843 spring season of lectures ended in early June, and the fall season began in late November.[36]

Although most Lyceums began with local lecturers, professionals soon established lecture circuits in the North. However, the South's low population density and underdeveloped transportation system made it unprofitable and difficult for prominent lecturers to present series of lectures. Furthermore, in the antebellum period many Southerners developed an antagonism to Northern lecturers. Nevertheless, Northern lecturers occasionally stopped in Montgomery and Mobile on their way to New Orleans. Also unlike the Northern practice, Montgomery's Lyceum never built its own lecture hall and library. Consequently the city's school system did not benefit from the Lyceum as did the educational systems of many Northern cities.[37]

Theoretically, the Lyceum had great potential for helping young members of the middling classes improve their positions, increasing the city's economic diversification, and galvanizing the intellectual life of the city. In general, the planters who dominated the South's economic and social systems had few intellectual interests, and the middling classes, the foundation of the Lyceum movement, were relatively weak in the South. Whereas members of the middling classes in the North aspired to better their positions within a solid middle group, members of the upper levels of the middling classes in Montgomery may have aspired to rise into the planter-dominated elite. Montgomery's Lyceum never had the practical, work ethic orientation of a movement intended to serve the aspirations of young mechanics, or artisans. They were so few in the South and had so little hope for economic success in a system that was basically hostile to skilled manual trades that there was little motivation for their participation in adult education. Furthermore, Montgomery's Lyceum was founded after the best years of the Lyceum movement in the South, the 1830s, and it followed the national trend away from the movement's original practical purpose of adult education and toward lectures oriented to sophisticated entertainment. Although Montgomery's Lyceum must have positively affected individual members, the Lyceum did not have an appreciable impact on the city as a whole.[38]

The Mechanics Association sponsored lectures similar to those of the Lyceum. George R. Glidden, an English archeologist and scholar, gave four lectures in May 1852, and the Reverend Andrew A. Lipscomb lectured on the "Southern Man" in January 1853. Such lectures hardly seem like suitable subjects for an association of skilled working men. By 1860 Montgomery had some two hundred mechanics and an additional two hundred clerks and bookkeepers, certainly sufficient numbers to have supported lectures tailored to their needs. But again, Montgomery's Mechanics Association was following national trends of mechanics' institutes toward topics of general rather than practical interest. The association's six-hundred volume library may have had more practical value for the membership.[39]

In the mid-1850s the Literary Club of Montgomery played an important role in the intellectual and social life of the city. The subject matter of the club's lectures, papers and debates indicates eclectic interests and taste: John Milton, Jonathan Swift, John Randolph and Aaron Burr. Members debated the usury law, the theater, modern civilization's restraint on the passion for military glory, and the adverse impact of democratic institutions on the refinement of taste, society and literature. The latter two subjects directly related to the Cult of Chivalry and the class distinctions that were becoming more pronounced in the 1850s. Those who lectured and presented papers were in the tradition of the gentlemen amateur. If the speakers were representative of the club's membership, the Literary Club provided a weekly gathering for planters, businessmen and professionals.[40]

Both men and women attended public lectures, and successful lecturers became celebrities. In the area of foreign affairs, a lecture on Cuba was given in April 1843, Polish exile Charles Lemanski spoke in March 1843, Hungarian patriot Louis Kossuth appeared in April 1852, and W. C. Catherwood lectured on Nicaragua in April 1856.[41] Montgomerians were not directly interested in events in Poland and Hungary, although they perhaps empathized with the political aspirations of oppressed nationalities. Discussions of Cuba and Nicaragua, of course, touched upon slavery, race, plantation agriculture and expansion.

Scientific or pseudoscientific subjects captured the imagination of antebellum audiences. Phrenology, one of the fads of the day, connected character with the shape and protuberances of the skull. America's geographic and socially mobile society highly valued a physical means to judge character. Moreover, phrenology offered "scientific" support for theories of white superiority shared by most white Americans. Aside from other lectures, Montgomerians heard two of the most famous promoters of phrenology, Lorenzo Niles Fowler and Samuel Roberts Wells. Professor Fowler and his brother wrote *Phrenology Proved, Illustrated, and Applied*, a book that went through thirty editions. Fowler and Wells conducted lucrative lecture tours in the United States, Canada, England, Scotland and Ireland, and continued to promote phrenology before unsuspecting audiences even after the "science" was discredited. The first of six nightly lectures beginning in late January 1858 was free; subsequent lectures were twenty-five cents each, indicating that the lectures were probably directed to large, general audiences rather than to select ones. Private examinations were also offered. Phrenology was not the only pseudoscience to appeal to audiences of the time. In March 1843, Professor Skelton, who gave Montgomery's first lecture on mesmerism, aroused public interest in what was thought of as a new science. Dr. Williams lectured and demonstrated experiments on psychology in March 1850, and Dr. C. A. Woodruff of Georgia gave a series of lectures on geology that November.

Assorted other lectures likewise edified Montgomerians. In May 1838 former member of Parliament James S. Buckingham delivered a series of lectures on Palestine before audiences of up to three hundred, which included prominent citizens of Montgomery and its environs. Asa Whitney, Connecticut merchant turned railroad promoter, spoke to both houses of the General Assembly in December 1847. After having visited China in 1840–41, he was convinced of the commercial benefits to the United States of trade with China. Whitney lobbied Congress and spoke to almost every state legislature as part of his seven-year campaign to get national support for building a transcontinental railroad by a Northern route—a project that conflicted with Southern political interests. In April 1859, a Dr. Nichols presented a series of lectures in which he refuted popular religious, moral, intellectual and political objections to Roman Catholicism—again positions contrary to the prevailing sentiments of the city. Dorothea Lynde Dix, the inspiration for the founding of thirty-eight mental hospitals, appealed to the Alabama General Assembly in 1849. The Alabama Insane Hospital was subsequently founded, in 1852, adjacent to the University of Alabama in Tuscaloosa, reputedly as belated compensation for that city's loss of the General Assembly some five years earlier.[42]

Nationally, the lecture phenomenon of the 1840s and 1850s was approved by those who believed leisure time should be used only for educational purposes. Ironically, however, the distinction between lectures' educational

> **CONCERT HALL:**
> ——o——
> **FOR THREE NIGHTS LONGER.**
> Will Positively Close on Wednesday, Dec. 14.
>
> ## DR. G. D. BEALE'S
> ## ENTERTAINMENTS!
>
> CONSISTING of some of the most Gorgeous Scenery ever presented to the public. NEW YORK HARBOR, with shipping of all nations.
>
> **DR. KANE'S ARCTIC REGIONS,**
> Being a voyage from New York to the open Polar Sea.
>
> **MOUNT VERNON,**
> The Home of Washington. Giving splendid views by day and night, with GRAND ILLUMINATION, VOCAL AND INSTRUMENTAL MUSIC.
>
> The whole to conclude with the
>
> **Mirth Provoking Italian Marionetts.**
>
> Exhibition every night at 7½ o'clock, and on Wednesday and Saturday afternoons, at 3 o'clock.
> nov26   DR. G. D. BEALE, Proprietor.

Newspaper advertisement for Concert Hall lectures and entertainment, Montgomery Daily Advertiser, *December 13, 1859.*

and entertaining aspects blurred. The tendency of lecturers to favor entertaining their audiences, rather than informing or persuading them, was criticized at the time. Late in the antebellum period, the strictures against public entertainment were relaxed.[43] None of these issues strongly affected the popularity of lectures—or commercial entertainment—in Montgomery, because opposition to entertainment was not as strong as in New England and the connection of lectures with the work ethic was relatively unimportant.

The city's intellectual life was not particularly extensive or rigorous, and, to a greater extent than in the North, was largely confined to more privileged white males. Lyceum, Literary Club and some of the public lecturers favored topics of interest to the privileged. The Mechanics Association and most public lecturers favored topics of interest to the general public. But lecturers and their subject matter were not choices made exclusively by privileged Montgomerians whose values, interests and needs did not coincide with those of the mechanics. The mechanics, especially if supplemented by clerks and bookkeepers, were numerous enough to have supported appropriate lectures had suitable lecturers been available. However, in the South, low population density and significant distances between towns of any size reduced the choice of lecturers. For financial reasons, lecturers favored regions with the greatest concentrated populations. Consequently, Montgomery had to depend on its own citizens to lecture. Many of the outside lecturers who did appear presented entertaining, commercially-oriented programs that attracted large general audiences rather than small specialized ones. Despite differences in audiences, speakers, frequency, subject matter and purposes, Montgomery's experience with lectures approximated that of the rest of antebellum America.

Secret fraternal societies filled very different needs than the literary societies. The leading fraternal organizations in Montgomery, as in the rest of antebellum America, were the Freemasons and the Odd Fellows. Montgomery's first Masonic lodge was organized in 1821 and chartered in 1823. Its officers were prominent citizens, a situation maintained throughout the period. Although the lodge's rituals and charitable works were shrouded in secrecy, it did conduct public ceremonies on the feast days of Freemasonry's Christian patrons: St. John the Baptist (June 24) and St. John the Divine (December 27). These events provided forums for explaining Freemasonry's objectives, chiefly the promotion of individual self-control and collective charity.[44]

In 1826, just three years after Montgomery's first Masonic lodge was chartered, anti-Masonic hysteria swept America. Many who believed that secret societies were conspiratorial believed that they helped maintain privilege and, more importantly, threatened republicanism. Nationally, more than half the Masons resigned from their lodges. Although no Alabamians organized an anti-Masonic political party, Alabama lodges were adversely affected almost immediately. In June 1826 one Montgomery Mason blamed public prejudice on ignorance, although he admitted that some members were unworthy. A Montgomery editor also admitted that discipline in most Masonic lodges had been lax and that many members were immoral, yet he questioned the decision of Tuscaloosa Methodists to exclude ministers and presiding elders associated with Freemasonry. The Montgomery lodge unquestionably suffered from anti-Masonic feelings: membership did not increase from its chartering in 1823 until it surrendered its charter in 1829. Alabama Freemasonry remained dormant for approximately a decade, until the Grand Lodge of Alabama finally reorganized in late 1836. The Montgomery lodge, rechartered in 1840, had seventy-five members by 1842, more than twice the membership of 1828. A second lodge, begun in 1852, attracted sixty members by the time of the Civil War. Both lodges were apparently composed of a cross-section of elite and middling classes. Although the original lodge admitted Jews, only one Christian minister was recorded on the membership rolls of either lodge during the entire antebellum period. The rapid growth of Alabama lodges in the mid-1850s elicited concern; in 1857 the Grand Master of the Grand Lodge complained that many of the new Masons were unworthy and that their moral character did not merit membership. Montgomery Freemasons played prominent roles in the state organization. The Grand Lodge was moved from Tuscaloosa to Montgomery in 1847, and the *Masonic Signet* was published in Montgomery from 1853.[45]

Montgomery's Independent Order of Odd Fellows held annual public celebrations to commemorate the introduction of the order into the United States from England, but its rituals, fellowship, and charity were secret. In the 1830s former Freemasons swelled the ranks of Odd Fellows lodges, but the formation of Montgomery's first lodge in 1845 was unrelated to this national phenomenon. Alabama's first German Odd Fellows lodge was chartered in Montgomery in 1854. The city had three lodges by 1859. Although membership included at least one large planter and banker, lodge officers were predominantly small merchants and mechanics, decidedly different from the officers of the two Freemason lodges. The Odd Fellows considered themselves allies of Christianity, accepting Roman Catholics as well as Protestants. Yet Montgomery's German lodge had Jewish officers, as did the oldest lodge, St. Paul's Encampment.[46]

As elsewhere in the United States, Montgomery's fraternal orders attracted some of the urban elite, but they primarily served middling sorts: professional men, middle and small merchants, and, in the case of the Odd Fellows, mechanics. The fraternal orders, indeed, helped define the boundaries of middle-class respectability. The phenomenal growth of these two fraternal orders and myriad others—to the point that by 1900 upwards of forty percent of American adult males belonged to a secret fraternal order—was built on the attractions of initiation and other rites, not on the attractions of friendship, fellowship, or business and social advancement. Initially both the Freemasons and the Odd Fellows were little more than drinking clubs, but by the 1840s they existed to perform elaborate, mysterious rites. The transformation of the Masons, whose pre-1830s rites were relatively insignificant, was in response to the anti-Masonic movement. In the 1830s Masonic lodges severely restricted drinking, and they completely banned it by the end of the antebellum period. In the 1830s former Freemasons, having quit their own lodges, introduced more elaborate rituals into the previously convivial Odd Fellows lodges that they joined. The Grand Master of the Grand Lodge of Alabama asserted that Masonry was not about ceremony, but that Masonry was a philosophy whose general principles must be studied; he was, however, asserting what should be, rather than what was. Ritual, and especially its attendant hierarchies, elaborate costumes and regalia, appealed to a people in a fluid social order. The men who joined the secret orders seem to have been seeking, if only subconsciously, definite stratification and distinctions that their society did not offer.[47]

VOLUNTEER MILITARY COMPANIES

The social hierarchy of the West was even more fluid than that of the East; men could sometimes achieve status by securing billets as officers in the militia or by joining a volunteer military company. The proliferation of military titles from the 1830s, noted by visiting Northerners and Europeans, was a part of the Cult of Chivalry.[48] In the spring of 1860, the young ladies of Montgomery presented the newly-formed Metropolitan Guards with its flag, which a speaker hailed as a

> ... token of their [the young ladies'] high appreciation of your gal-

lantry, and . . . their confidence in your honor as men and your courage as soldiers . . . [The flag] . . . would evoke a spirit of chivalry in the South disinterested and self-sacrificing as that which animated the steel-clad knights who followed Richard of the Lion-Heart to the Holy Land, and fierce and untamable as that which gave a deathless frame to [Prince] Rupert and his cavaliers . . . but when accepted by freemen as the alternative of national ruin, and degradation, it becomes a holy work—develops the most god-like attributes of our nature—and furnishes the golden opportunity for making those bright records of human achievement which posterity delights to contemplate.[49]

The young officer who accepted the banner responded that

. . . we will cherish it as a sacred treasure—we will guard it as the vestal priestess did the sacred flame at Rome, and we will protect it as we would our household gods. "Never will foul dishonor blur our name," nor shall we ever permit one single stain to soil its bright escutcheon.[50]

The militia in Alabama predated statehood. An 1807 Mississippi Territory law established a militia command and an organizational structure, provided for periodic musters, and called for local companies composed of white males between the ages of sixteen and fifty, who were obliged to arm themselves. The new state of Alabama retained the same militia structure, although modifications made in 1821 allowed each militia regiment to raise a volunteer company with distinctive privileges. After 1837, when removal of the Creeks lessened the need for a state military force, Alabama reduced expenses by promoting volunteer companies that received limited state support. Militia musters were reduced to two annually, but volunteers were required to drill six to twelve times a year. Volunteers were exempt from some civic responsibilities, such as road work, jury and patrol duty. Although the militia generally was associated with ineptitude and public drunkenness and the volunteer companies with social activities and aspirations, Montgomery's military units took military functions seriously and frequently volunteered to serve outside the state.[51]

Portrait photograph of Edmund McCurdy Hastings in Montgomery True Blues uniform, 1840s or 1850s. Hastings was born in Lancaster County, Pennsylvania, in 1811, and died in Montgomery in 1870.

Montgomery's first volunteer company, the Montgomery Light Infantry, founded in 1824, was led by Montgomery merchants who were natives of the Northeast, not the South. A physician, H. W. Henry, commanded the second volunteer company, the Montgomery Huzzars or Henry's Horse Company. The state did not incorporate the unit until 1832, some five years after its organization. The Montgomery Blues, the city's most prominent volunteer company, formed on February 20, 1836, to serve against the Seminoles in Florida. Two days later the Montgomery [County] Invincibles were organized. Both companies served with distinction at the Battle of Thlonotosassa Creek in April 1836. Although their captain volunteered them, the Blues initially refused to serve in the Mexican War because no Alabama troops had been called. Several local volunteer companies ultimately served in the Mexican

War: the Relief Volunteers, the Mount Meigs Cavalry and the Montgomery Dragoons. None saw action, although individuals sometimes fought in other units. The Invincibles became the Rough and Ready Invincibles in 1849; the Alabama Dragoons and the Montgomery Rifle Corps or Riflemen formed in 1854. The Metropolitan Guards organized in 1859 and the Montgomery Greys in 1860. Alabama's military act of 1860, which increased taxes on those who did not serve, may have spurred participation in Montgomery's volunteer companies.[52]

With the exception of the Montgomery Blues, which existed continuously, volunteer military companies arose in response to crises: Alabama, Florida and Texas in 1836, Oregon and Mexico in 1846, Kansas in 1856, and John Brown's Raid in 1859. The Blues served important social functions, lending color and pomp to civic ceremonies such as the Fourth of July and Washington's Birthday, which the Blues erroneously celebrated as their organizational day. They hosted balls and strawberry suppers, received tributes from other Montgomery organizations, and exchanged visits with elite volunteer companies from other cities. The Blues bivouacked in 1856 with Columbus and Macon volunteer companies at LaGrange, Georgia,

Joseph Thoits Moore (1828–54) painting of the Montgomery True Blues on parade, Market Street (today's Dexter Avenue) with the Montgomery Hall hotel and several mercantile houses as the background, c. 1853.

Painting of the Montgomery True Blues at Camp Owen, near old Augusta, with the railroad in the foreground, 1853.

to attend the commencement of the Southern Female College, whose literary society had made the Blues honorary members. Parades, drills, musters, marksmanship contests and encampments attracted considerable attention from the city's citizens, especially the young ladies.[53] On the eve of the Civil War, the Montgomery Blues' muster roll recorded four officers (two merchants, a lawyer and a clerk), a surgeon, and seventy-one men, the majority of whom were solid members of the middling classes. Fourteen were Northern born; two were natives of Bavaria.[54]

Volunteer fire companies had similar social and civic functions. The first company emerged in January 1831, a hook and ladder company followed in 1843, and a fire engine company was started in 1847. The companies held torchlight parades from their fire houses, mounted fireworks displays, and hosted balls and champagne dinners.[55] Fellow citizens honored firemen as "noble-hearted men banded together, not for the advancement of their own private interests, but for the preservation of the lives and property of others."[56] Left unsaid was that volunteer service also exempted men from unheralded duty in the bucket brigades, alongside all other Montgomery males, black and white. Volunteer firemen were also exempted from jury and militia duty from 1848, and after seven years' service, they became honorary members with all the rights of active members. Each company limited membership (seventy-five in the Dexter Fire Company, for example), and applicants could be rejected by three blackballs. Several of the city's richest planters, the sheriff, and members of the upper middling classes joined fire companies. As prominent Roman Catholic and Jewish businessmen were also included, civic status was not narrowly restricted to the city's overwhelmingly Protestant majority. Members pulled engines to fires, pumped engines by hand, and afterwards cleaned the engines and "pipes." Montgomery experienced the rivalry among volunteer fire companies that was so prevalent in the nineteenth century. Two years after the three companies united under a city fire chief in 1858, the rivalries were under control.[57]

In addition to fraternal orders and volunteer military and fire companies, Montgomerians belonged to agricultural, religious, temperance, literary, lecture, library and social associations. They provided services, pursued social reform, and staged charity and cultural events. Individuals belonged for a variety of reasons, including to establish a place within the community and its social hierarchy. Voluntary associations helped establish order and aided in defining respectable uses of leisure time. Voluntary associations were locally controlled and, therefore, could more easily conform to local needs and values than commercial entertainment, which was then coming to dominate American leisure activities. Regional and national businessmen controlled commercial entertainment, which eventually homogenized American culture. Commercial entertainment also led many Americans to enjoy their leisure time passively as spectators. But active participation and local control characterized most of Montgomery's leisure activities throughout the antebellum period.

2

Seasonal Amusements and Diversions

The agricultural cycle and long oppressive summers shaped leisure activities in antebellum Montgomery. The extended fall-winter holiday season, the Fourth of July, racing meets and, for the wealthy, summers spent at resorts enriched the year and marked the passing of time. The everyday pastimes that were so important in establishing and maintaining a community were thoroughly integrated with seasonal amusements. Like everyday pastimes, seasonal amusements reveal that Montgomerians' values, tastes, experiences and social practices both coincided and conflicted with the behavior of their fellow Americans, North and South.

During the antebellum period, seasonal amusements changed from an essentially shared culture with an egalitarian veneer to a more diverse culture with more apparent taste and class distinctions. This change occurred, in part, because a larger population could sustain a variety of leisure activities, and because better transportation allowed more commercial entertainment to reach Montgomery. These forces shaped Montgomery, as they did much of the country.

Holidays

Montgomerians celebrated several patriotic holidays, most notably the Fourth of July, along with religious and seasonal ones like Thanksgiving, Christmas and New Year's. Late fall and early winter, when holidays clustered together, became a "season" by the 1850s. Montgomery's population reached its annual peak during the months after the cotton harvest. The wealthy who had summered outside the city, sometimes far away, returned, and transients further swelled the population. Planters and farmers who brought their crops to Montgomery lingered to enjoy theatrical, musical, minstrel and circus performances, as well as racing meets and the state agricultural fair. During the extended holiday season, the General Assembly convened and various state denominational and fraternal associations held their conventions.[1]

Numerous promoters, taking advantage of the swollen population, mounted exhibits. These included patriotic and religious paintings and projected or illuminated panoramic views of such sights as the Arctic, New York harbor and Mount Vernon—the latter's popularity was heightened by the fund drive to save George Washington's house as part of the national patrimony. Occasionally exhibitions were accompanied by vocal and instrumental music or supplemented with humorous marionette shows. The most elaborate of these occurred in December 1854 with the exhibition of sixty life-size paintings illustrating *Pilgrim's Progress*, John Bunyan's religious allegory. Of the six nationally-known artists whose paintings were displayed, only Frederick Edwin Church is widely admired today, but at the time Jasper Francis Cropsey enjoyed both an American and European reputation. *Mercy's Dream*, Daniel Huntington's contribution to this exhibition, attracted such public acclaim that it was reproduced and sold as an engraving. The American Art-Union helped build the public's taste for the fine arts through such artistic exhibitions, as well as the subscription sale of steel engravings of genre and landscape paintings done by American artists. At a dollar each, the etchings were too expensive for many Montgomerians.[2]

Beginning in 1855, the annual Alabama State Agricultural Society Fair added to the holiday season's entertainment diversity. The fairgrounds just north of the city included an amphitheater that seated ten thousand and an "Industrial Palace" with over fourteen thousand square feet of exhibition space, plus areas for livestock. The thirty-acre complex was one of the finest fairgrounds in the South. Planters and farmers displayed a great variety of breeds of horses, cattle, sheep, swine and poultry. They also exhibited corn, cotton and wheat, but the lateness of the season limited fruits and flowers. Although agricultural exhibits predominated, Alabama manufacturers showed agricultural implements and a variety of other locally-made goods. As many as fifty committees judged animal and horticultural entries, Alabama manufactures, and the numerous practical and decorative items made by women participants. The disproportionate number of prizes taken by local competitors indicates that participation may not have been very

Two scenes from the Alabama State Fair—top, the Amphitheatre; bottom, the Tilt—both from sketches by Nixon and published in Harper's Weekly, *November 27, 1858. The fourth annual fair of the Alabama State Agricultural Society took place November 1–6, 1858.*

widespread. Such fairs, which were popular throughout the country, were intended to stimulate agricultural improvement, but they also became great spectator entertainment and provided opportunities for socializing. By the time Alabama's fair was established, fairs throughout the country had added diverse attractions to their agricultural exhibits.[3]

The annual fairs catered to varied interests. Impressive opening ceremonies emphasized the importance of the fair—and of agriculture and manufacturing—to the state. A volunteer military company and a brass band escorted the governor and legislators to the opening ceremonies. Prominent Southerners were guest speakers. Large crowds from throughout Alabama and western and southern Georgia attended the six annual fairs. In 1855 six to seven thousand people attended, and in 1856 some twelve thousand attended on one day alone. To avoid brawls and murders, which occurred at fairs in Virginia and Tennessee, police patrolled the grounds in 1857. Commercial and agricultural exhibits attracted many men, but other activities attracted large numbers of men and women. These included plowing contests and trotting or harness racing at the fairgrounds' half-mile track. Plowing contests had categories for black and white men and boys; the prize for each of the four categories was five dollars. The fairs also included a midway with the usual array of human and animal curiosities.

In addition to exhibits that highlighted the state's agricultural and manufacturing diversity, such as it was, numerous popular entertainments, like equestrian demonstrations by local ladies and gentlemen, appealed to the more refined. From 1857 the fair offered an event that epitomized the South's self-identification with the Age of Chivalry: young gentlemen pitted their equestrian skills against one another in a tilt, a tournament of knights. Accompanied by heralds, and dressed in costumes with plumes and scarves, several "knights" competed for a set of lady's jewelry valued at one hundred dollars. Ironically, the champion of the first of these tournaments was not of the landed elite, but a son of William Knox, an Irish immigrant and one of Montgomery's wealthiest businessmen, and a sometime planter. The young man presented his prize to the beautiful Miss LeVert of Mobile, a belle, but again, not of the landed elite.

This Montgomery tournament fell short of the ideal: several of the participating young gentlemen's titles—the Wild Knight, the Knight of Mount Vernon, the Knight of Alabama, and especially the victor's title, Knight Charles O'Malley—lacked the ring of medieval romance. Young Knox's "title" was based on Charles Lever's 1840 novel of the same name; the very popular story portrayed the spirited life of the British army and Irish society—aristocratic, but hardly conforming to Sir Walter Scott's ideal of chivalry. Furthermore, the prize, one hundred dollars worth of jewelry, rather than the customary practice of the victor crowning his young lady as the Queen of Love and Beauty, smacked of crass materialism.

The tournament surely had been intended to display Southern gentility. The Cult of Chivalry, a peculiarly Southern manifestation of the Romantic Movement that had swept the country, was characterized by idealization of women, gentlemanly honor, elaborate manners, hospitality, dueling, and equestrian activities such as hunting, racing and tournaments. The latter, copied from Virginia and South Carolina where they were highly developed, clearly illustrated a fascination with the past and an identification with feudalism. As such, Southern romanticism and the Cult of Chivalry, to the extent that it really existed, rejected the Northern ideal of the merchant-prince and crude commercialism—the actual source of the wealth of many of Montgomery's elite. Romanticism in none of its forms was characterized by rationalism; it was, after all, a rejection of cold classicism.[4]

Thanksgiving, Christmas and New Year's also fell during the extended holiday season. Thanksgiving, established by the federal government in 1789, seems to have been a minor holiday. Early in the antebellum period, Christmas also was probably kept as a simple family affair; in 1828 a sentimental editorial described an intimate observance with an extended family gathered around the fireside. In 1836 Alabama became the first state to establish Christmas as a legal holiday. Christmas acquired more elaborate aspects, at least for those with the wherewithal to celebrate more elaborately. It was celebrated with church services, and eating and drinking, but gift giving acquired an increasingly important place in the celebration.[5] In the depressed economy of 1857, the editor of the *Montgomery Weekly Journal* urged parents to assure their children that although there might not be "extravagant expenditures . . . and costly gifts, as in years past" that

Christmas could be enjoyed with "hilarious games, and in time-honored pastimes, and perchance, in a few dances." Montgomerians did not burn Yule logs or hang mistletoe, but they did enjoy "the genuine Saxon usage of eating and drinking 'good cheer.'"[6] Christmas observance was not confined to religious and family activities. In some years, theatrical performances, horse races, and bird shooting contests provided entertainment on Christmas Day.[7] Economic hard times notwithstanding, in 1857 "The 'Cowbellians' [a group of gentlemen revelers] were out in all of their glory and noise on Christmas Eve, unceremoniously invading any house that happened to be open and eating and drinking of the good things to be found."[8]

Some Montgomerians celebrated New Year's with revels. In 1855 the Strikers, another group of gentlemen revelers, presented a masquerade with "statuary" of gladiators, discus throwers, wrestlers, charioteers, equestrians and knights coming to life.[9] The cold and drizzle did not deter the Cowbellians on New Year's Eve 1860; dressed "very fantastic and amusing" as kings, princes, potentates, knights, sailors and Ethiopians, they made "s" on their friends.[10] Predominantly Protestant Montgomery imported these carnival customs from Roman Catholic Mobile—where they eventually became the foundations of that city's Mardi Gras celebration—and combined them with traditional and more respectable observances.

The city's affluent kept open house on New Year's Day for their friends and acquaintances. Hosts offered their guests meats and oysters, cakes and candies, fruit, and drink. Although keeping open house conformed to the Southern ideal of hospitality, the practice was not confined to the South. New Year's Day open house was especially popular in Northern cities.[11] In the mid-1850s Montgomerians altered the custom of keeping open house.

> Our city, according to a recently imported custom from New England, we believe, will be today signalized by universal visiting, pop-calling, and wine drinking. It is this rule that every body calls at every residence where he, or she, is acquainted, remaining a minute or two, leaves a card, and by this short and easy process is considered a visitor, and entitled to an invitation to general parties. It is a goodly custom and very convenient to persons of little leisure or disposition to visit.

We have heard of some efforts to kill off, and put into desuetude this goodly custom, but we suppose it will be generally observed, and that most, if not all, of our ladies will receive today.[12]

The "recently imported custom" elicited some resistance, probably because it provided an entree for those who normally were not received by the city's elite or those who may not have recognized the solidifying class lines. Furthermore, the very short "pop calls" hardly conformed to the true ideals of genteel hospitality. At the time, however, hospitality and noblesse oblige appear to have proved stronger than socioeconomic distinctions regarding open house.

Numerous grand balls punctuated the extended holiday season. Individuals and, more frequently, voluntary associations, including volunteer military companies and social and hunting clubs, sponsored these balls.[13] Dancing, which was of course the chief activity of the balls, was popular throughout the period. Dancing teachers and schools were required because Montgomerians were not just dancing the Virginia Reel, the Cotillion and waltzes, but a large number of fashionable dances and complicated figures, such as the Gallop Quadrille, L'Esmeralda, La Tarantelle, La Sicilienne, Mazurka and Mascowiska. Dancing schools, the first of which opened in the 1820s, taught children and adults the popular dances of the day. Adult dancing school students must have had the luxury of ample free time, because the dancing schools gave lessons for adults during weekday mornings or mid-afternoons.[14] The poor, of course, did not learn the latest fashionable dances or attend grand balls, but neither did all Montgomerians who could well have afforded to attend. The Baptist and Methodist churches condemned dancing and public amusement. Beginning in 1845, the Presbyterian Church expelled a prominent physician several times for dancing, attending a public ball, drunkenness, and using profane language. In 1856 the physician left the Presbyterian Church for the Episcopal Church. But even there, the bishop who confirmed him disapproved of dancing and would not confirm dancing teachers.[15] Considering the popularity of the balls and the fact that Montgomery supported at least two dancing teachers from about 1830, church disapproval appears to have had little effect.[16]

Although poor whites and those who strictly adhered to the tenets of their churches did not attend assemblies, or grand balls, some of Montgomery's slaves did. In 1853 Frederick Law Olmsted, then a *New York Times* correspondent, observed a Montgomery assembly put on by slaves.

> During the winter, the negroes, in Montgomery, have their "assemblies," or dress balls, which are got up "regardless of expense," in very grand style. Tickets are advertised to these balls, "admitting one gentleman and two ladies, $1;" and "Ladies are assured that they may rely on the strictest order and propriety being observed." Cards of invitation, finely engraved with handsome vignettes, are sent, not only to the fashionable slaves, but to some of the more esteemed white people, who, however, take no part, except as lookers-on. All the fashionable dances are executed; no one is admitted, except in full dress; there are regular masters of ceremonies, floor committees, etc.; and a grand supper always forms a part of the entertainment.[17]

This description not only suggests what white assemblies must have been like, but it also indicates some gradation within the slave population—"the fashionable slaves." Olmsted explained how some of the slaves learned "all the fashionable dances." An enterprising Montgomery slave, a carpenter by trade and a building contractor as well, conducted a slave dancing school two nights a week. Slave dancing students paid for their lessons.[18]

Socially sanctioned activities in which members of lower strata imitated the behavior of their betters or in which the social order was inverted (most often associated with pre-Lent or carnival celebrations) served as an emotional release. More importantly, it reinforced the notion that the prevailing order was natural and preferable. For these reasons, Montgomery's civic authorities and slave owners sanctioned the slave assemblies. However, when relaxation of slave control threatened rather than reinforced the prevailing order, city authorities restricted slave holiday celebrations. Because of the threat of a slave insurrection, in December 1856 the city council forbade slave assemblies without permission of the council. The mayor requested that planters not give their slaves passes to stay in the city after dark. On

December 22 the council rejected a petition of the black band for permission to give an assembly on Christmas Day. Four years later, the discovery of another slave insurrection plot, to have been initiated on Christmas Eve, caused a great deal of excitement: the guard paraded in the streets in the evenings, and slave assemblies were again cancelled. At this time, flyers inciting the slaves to rebel were discovered in each of the recently delivered copies of the popular *Godey's Lady's Book*. Neither of these incidents was considered serious enough, however, to divert the white population from its holiday celebrations.[19]

The extended holiday season included the anniversary of Andrew Jackson's victory at New Orleans, an event of particular importance in the Old Southwest, as well as the birthdays of George Washington and Benjamin Franklin. The latter was a private affair of the Typographical Society held in the city's finest hotel, whereas the Jackson and Washington celebrations had both private and public aspects. Attendance was limited at assemblies and dinners, but the outdoor activities were for all. They included cannon salutes, prayers, orations, military parades, and parades of citizens and civic officials on foot and in carriages. The military character of the celebration of Washington's birthday became more prominent in the 1850s with military assemblies and dinners and visits by volunteer military companies from as far away as Macon, Georgia.[20]

Nationally, parades captivated Americans of the 1850s, and local militia companies invariably participated. But volunteer military companies dominated patriotic celebrations in Montgomery. Other than the volunteer fire companies (and the circuses, of course), no organizations could provide the color and excitement of the city's military companies. The Freemasons could provide some color, but they conducted their own parades in December and June. By the end of the antebellum period, as the grip of romanticism and Southern nationalization tightened, military trappings had captured the imaginations of Montgomerians.[21]

The Fourth of July was the most important civic celebration during the country's antebellum period. It followed a fairly set format with a parade, a public prayer to the "Throne of Grace," a reading of the Declaration of Independence, and patriotic speeches. Celebratory picnics, dinners or barbecues, grand balls or ordinary dances, and perhaps fireworks followed the more formal observation of Independence Day. As early as 1821, Montgomery was following the standard observation: a cannon salute signaled the beginning of the day and later a second salute announced the public celebration. Following the public observation, Montgomerians continued to celebrate. The more influential gentlemen adjourned to a local tavern for a dinner enlivened by patriotic songs and patriotic or topical toasts.[22]

In 1832 the solidarity of the earlier years had vanished, and the city was divided over the national election. Each of the three separate celebrations, representing differing political persuasions, followed the customary format of invocation, reading of the Declaration and an oration.[23] After a grand celebration in 1851 in which the military flavor dominated, observation of the Fourth of July declined in importance.[24]

In 1860, however, two large, separate celebrations marked the occasion. One of the events was formal and had political overtones. The Montgomery Blues, Metropolitan Guards, Mounted Rifles, and visiting Wetumpka Light Guards marched to the fairgrounds. A large crowd of ladies and gentlemen filled the amphitheater to hear a volunteer military company lieutenant deliver an oration and a private read the Declaration of Independence. The formal celebration having ended, the immense crowd feasted on barbecue.[25]

In addition to the fairground celebration of the Fourth, some eight hundred to a thousand "pleasure seekers" celebrated the day in Charles Linn's private gardens and groves just a mile from the city. (Perhaps Linn, a forty-six year old Swedish immigrant who had grown rich as a Montgomery merchant, wanted to recognize his debt to the United States for his material success.) This event seems to have been a real community celebration. Black and white, young and old, and members of all strata of society attended. A brass band marched around the grounds; a group of German vocalists entertained the crowd. Several adolescent "gentlemen" participated in a speaking contest. The host himself gave a short autobiographical speech. Refreshments followed these more formal aspects. Someone prematurely released the greased pig who promptly wreaked havoc among those having refreshments. The day's events included jumping, sack racing, and greased pole climbing.[26]

Montgomery celebrated its holidays, in private and in public, in much the same way as did the rest of the country. In an age of intense patriotism, celebration of patriotic holidays helped define the country's common heritage. At the end of the antebellum period, however, sectional feelings and sectional interpretations of the issues of the American Revolution may have defined a diverse, rather than a common heritage. How Montgomery celebrated the Fourth of July and the extended holiday season also reveals increased divisions among the various strata of society as they became more rigid. This was not unique to the South. During the antebellum period, slave assemblies were unique to the South, but aspects of other holiday activities—especially the tournaments and the ever-present volunteer military companies—reveal a city influenced by the Romantic Movement and Southern sectionalism, a city whose leisure activities resembled those of the North, but also displayed subtle differences.

Horse Racing

Except in New England, where the popularity of horse racing was limited, thoroughbred racing enjoyed popularity throughout antebellum America, especially in the South where it was associated with the ideal of the country gentleman. Consequently, breeding and racing thoroughbreds had social implications. Racing meets provided opportunities to display the exaggerated manners of the elite, especially for those with social aspirations. Racing meets, like "pop calls," gave social access to the elite, particularly to young ladies, that was otherwise limited. Racing also offered opportunities to gamble, but that too was associated with the tradition of the gentleman. Horse racing enjoyed a degree of popularity in Montgomery and its hinterland during most of the antebellum period. Although horses were raced throughout the year, thoroughbred racing meets were generally held during the extended holiday season and, much less frequently, in the spring.

Informal racing occurred from the earliest days of settlement. The fourth recorded Montgomery ordinance, January 1820, prohibited horse racing in the streets. Apparently the five dollar fine was inadequate to stop the practice, because in 1829 the council passed a more detailed anti-racing ordinance, and in 1835 raised the fine to as much as forty dollars and as many as twenty-five lashes for slaves.[27] Yet spirited men continued unorganized or spontaneous racing for competition, betting, and the sheer excitement of the race.

Aside from racing in the streets, formal, organized meets began at least as early as 1821.[28] Before an April 1826 meet, "A Friend of the Turf" commented that it was

> . . . a matter of surprise to many, that a good mile track has not been made in the flourishing town of Montgomery, surrounded, as it is, by young men of fortune, and wealthy planters. Judges pronounce the soil well adapted to the course, and almost every class of citizen is interested in having one established.[29]

The writer also noted that horse racing, "unlike many other sports," was "unattended with cruelty," and that merchants, tavern keepers and farmers would benefit from an established course. At the time Montgomery had races and several race courses, but apparently not well established ones. As early as December 1828 spectators came from a hundred miles away to attend a four-day meet, the first meet in Montgomery attended by a large number of ladies in carriages.[30] Racing meets were becoming respectable.

By the 1830s thoroughbred racing became the country's first popular spectator sport. During the 1830s and 1840s, the most important decades for antebellum horse racing, national leaders like Andrew Jackson, John C. Calhoun, Henry Clay and John Quincy Adams, were enthusiastic about the turf.[31] Racing's growing popularity depended less on an interest in horseflesh and improved breeding, than on gambling and, for the elite and those with social aspirations, the association of racing with gentility. The popularity of racing in Alabama followed the national trend. *Spirit of the Times*, the New York weekly that reported on sports and the theater, noted in 1836 that Alabama jockey clubs paid large purses, and that those of the jockey club of Mobile were exceeded only by those of Charleston, which was then the horse racing capital of the country. Although not in the league of Mobile, racing in Montgomery and the Black Belt was thriving. Racing meets were held at nearby tracks at Mount Meigs east of Montgomery and at Haynesville, Lowndesboro and Benton to the west. Dallas County even further west was noted for fine racing.[32]

Montgomery's jockey club was organized in July 1828. Throughout the period, the club's officers included prominent citizens of the town and its environs. The jockey club, which did not have its own race track, used the privately-owned Bertrand Course.[33] In 1838, a special correspondent for the *Spirit of the Times* praised the proprietors for their work in promoting horse racing and wrote that the new ladies' stand was "for convenience and neatness of style . . . surpassed by none in the Union."[34] Another correspondent considered the new seventeen thousand dollar complex "one of the handsomest establishments in the country;" its club stand, he noted, was only equaled by the new ladies' pavilion in Charleston.[35]

The jockey club advertised for several months before the Bertrand Course five-day meet that was to begin on Christmas Eve Day, 1839. Such advertisements attracted spectators from the hinterland and regional competitors for the large purses.[36] Thoroughbred racing, ostensibly a sport of gentlemen, was actually a national commercial enterprise. Reporting on the February 1841 meet, the senior editor of the *Spirit of the Times* referred to "this fine course," the "good people of Montgomery and vicinity," and large crowds, including ladies—and ankle deep mud from six weeks of continuous rain.[37]

Although the jockey club sponsored regular winter meets at the Bertrand Course, racing's popularity declined. Thoroughbred racing, with its elite associations, was challenged by egalitarian trotting or harness racing, and thoroughbred racing subsequently declined nationally. In Montgomery thoroughbred racing essentially died out in the 1850s. In July 1852, a large crowd assembled for a trotting race run by local horses, but the course at that time had already grown up with grass. *The Spirit of the Times* recorded only one race in 1853, a one-day trotting race in late May, and no races in 1854, 1855 and 1856.[38]

In 1857 thoroughbred racing was revived in Montgomery. David H. Carter built a new race course beyond the fairgrounds north of the city, within a quarter of a mile of the river, and near the railroad depot. The extensive facilities had a judges' stand, two-story ladies' stand, and two-story public stand. Accommodations for the horses included spring and well water and a covered horse walk surrounding each of the seven large stables, which had a total capacity of approximately forty horses. The flat track itself followed the layout of Charleston's Washington Course with two straight quarter-mile stretches and two quarter-mile curves. Judges from Charleston, New York, Boston, Mobile and New Orleans praised the new course. Carter intended that Montgomery supplant Charleston as the premier race city in the South, if not in the country.[39] But his commercial venture failed, as had at least four earlier Montgomery race tracks.

Although a minority was passionately attracted to horse racing, especially thoroughbred racing, commercial racing that involved shipment of horses throughout the United States could not be maintained without sustained popular support. Several promising starts encouraged Montgomery's jockey club and race track proprietors, but repeatedly, bad weather, competition from other types of entertainment, and opposition to racing and the gambling associated with it frustrated their high hopes.

The overwhelming number of Bertrand Course races were run in December, and Carter Course races in November, December, and January. Although having racing meets from November through January helped ensure larger potential audiences, bad weather and competition from other entertainment decreased that audience. The extended holiday season attracted a wide variety of commercial entertainments. Of these, circuses presented the greatest challenge. Horse racing could not compete successfully with circus showmanship and spectacle, especially if children were involved. Moreover, circuses were mounted under cover, an important consideration during the season.

Bad weather repeatedly plagued fall and winter meets. Cold and rain deterred crowds, and rain made the track heavy and slow. Despite the engineering precautions taken in constructing the Carter track, it could not cope with heavy rains. Meets usually lasted five days; bad weather interfered with at least one day of approximately half of the Montgomery meets reported in the *Spirit of the Times* between 1836 and 1860. Cold and inclement weather, as well as slow running times, discouraged all but the most avid racing enthusiasts.

For horse racing to succeed in Montgomery, a large portion of the potential audience had to support the sport. Elsewhere in the country, the introduction of trotting or harness racing had broadened the appeal of horse racing. The middling classes in the East enjoyed trotting, which was relatively inexpensive and mostly uncontaminated by betting. Trotting even flourished in New England, where thoroughbred racing had failed to arouse much interest. In early December 1851, the Bertrand Course mounted its first trotting race, some fourteen years after trotting first appeared in the South at Mobile. Subsequently almost half the racing meets in Montgomery were trotting races. But as trotting became the sport of the people, the elite lost interest in horse racing. Viewing trotting as too common, the elite left the new sport to the middling classes.[40]

In addition to class associations that hampered the commercial success of thoroughbred horse racing throughout the country, especially in the Northeast, evangelical churches denounced the sport; they found the betting particularly offensive. Montgomery's churches, however, do not appear to have voiced strong opposition.[41] In 1840 a resolution of Montgomery's Baptist Church condemned "places of public amusement and of doubtful character, such as the theatre, circus, and such like places."[42] Racing meets, presumably, qualified as "such like places," but opposition to horse racing certainly did not receive the attention given to the theater.

Nevertheless, the questionable respectability of horse racing affected attendance. Some newspapers tried to counter criticism of the turf. In 1838 a special correspondent to the *Spirit of the Times* reported that Montgomery

> . . . was thronged with strangers, and the citizens traveled out almost en masse to lend their aid to the proprietors, and to evince by their presence the satisfaction with which they regard the organization of a [jockey] Club which comprises a large portion of all the gentlemen of character and wealth in Montgomery and its vicinity. Not the slightest accident occurred during the meeting, nor any circumstance calculated to disturb the harmony and good feelings which characterized it.[43]

Local newspapermen also touted horse racing. The editor of the *Montgomery Mail*, who also served as an officer in the jockey club, promoted horse racing through his newspaper.⁴⁴ Yet racing's image was marred by rowdiness and gambling; the interrelated issues seem to have been respectability and social control of the middling and lower classes. If gentlemen controlled the course and ladies attended the races, criticism might be diverted.

At the November 1858 meeting of the Montgomery Jockey Club, several prominent gentlemen who were "desirous to advance the respectability of the institution" began planning to purchase the Carter Course. They intended "by their character and influence, [to] establish the sport in this vicinity on a favorable and reputable basis."⁴⁵ The following spring, these men, led by General Cornelius Robinson of Lowndes County, gathered forty subscribers who bought the racecourse of approximately one hundred twenty acres for ten thousand dollars. The association, chartered by the state legislature in January 1860, reorganized the Montgomery Jockey Club; membership overlapped, but the latter group did not have a financial interest in the racecourse. General Robinson was also the president of the club; Colonel L. W. Hunter and General Hugh Park Watson were vice presidents. Membership of both association and club included some of the most prominent men in the community. The association mounted spring and fall meets.⁴⁶ In November 1860, the *Montgomery Weekly Post* said that horse racing was "becoming popular with our best citizens," and that the meet just concluded was "attended by the beauty and fashion of the county, as well as by its chivalry and gallantry."⁴⁷

The presence of ladies at racing meets lent respectability to a sport often marred by open gambling and associated with undesirable elements. As early as 1828, ladies attended the racing meets; later both the Bertrand and Carter courses had special stands for ladies. Newspaper accounts attributed increased decorum and reduced rowdiness to the presence of large numbers of ladies.⁴⁸ The secretary of the Montgomery Jockey Club, wrote to the *Spirit of the Times*:

> The decorum would have been creditable to any assembly. We attribute this to the presence of a large number of ladies, to whom the Jockey Club owe a thousand thanks . . . one of the most pleasant and decorous racing meetings ever held in Alabama. The attendance was every day large beyond

precedent, the ladies' stand being crowded.[49]

The ladies seemed to enjoy themselves thoroughly. "We never yet saw a lady of sense and feeling who could quietly sit in her chair, while the high-mettled coursers—princely in blood and almost human in ambition—fought the swift inches of the Homestretch. And we count on the ladies!"[50] The presence of ladies did not necessarily rule out fisticuffs. On one occasion a judge and an interested party got into a fight over a decision. Bystanders intervened, but the judge's wife "rose in her carriage and called at the top of her voice to let them alone, that she knew her husband could whip any man in Montgomery County and she wanted to see him do it."[51]

By 1861 declining popularity finished thoroughbred racing in the North, even on Long Island, New York, which had once been a national racing center. Trotting races influenced the elite to turn to other equestrian events from which the middling classes could be excluded, and other entertainment competed for the leisure time of the elite.[52] In Montgomery, however, the end of the antebellum period marked the high point of all types of commercial entertainment: theater, musical performances, minstrels, circuses and racing. Montgomery Jockey Club's 1860 fall meet was highly successful—and the last racing meet of the jockey club.[53] The success of Montgomery's last antebellum racing meet could indicate that racing had been accepted as respectable by the more religious elements in population. Horse racing, which was also associated with the idealized view of the Southern gentleman, could have allied itself with Southern sectionalism. Neither of these possibilities, however, are likely explanations of the final meet's success. The majority of Montgomery's white population would not have long deviated so radically from the national rejection of racing. More than likely, the successful season was merely another example of the occasional popularity of the turf exhibited earlier in the period. More importantly, the momentous political events of the fall of 1860 spurred public activity of all sorts; this mood seems to have been reflected in Montgomery's last antebellum racing season.

Summering at Mineral Springs

Of all antebellum leisure activities, summering away from Montgomery provided the most visible indicator of status. More than Greek Revival and Italianate mansions and conspicuous consumption and display, having the leisure from labor to flee Montgomery's oppressive summer heat distinguished the truly affluent from all lesser folk. Planters with both country and town houses usually spent only the cooler months in Montgomery. Some merchants conducted their business in the North or abroad during the summer. Some families summered just to the north of Montgomery, where they could come into town when necessary. In other families, the men stayed in the city and joined their families when their business schedules permitted. The most affluent could afford for all family members to spend the entire summer away from Montgomery. The exodus typically began in early June and extended through August. Gulf Coast resorts offered relief for a few families, but most frequented mineral springs.[54]

Beginning in the mid-1820s, watering places advertised widely in Montgomery newspapers. Montgomerians frequented Blount Springs, Warm Springs, Bladon Springs, Talladega White Sulphur Springs, Butler Springs, Valhermoso Springs and Shelby Springs in Alabama and Indian Springs, White Sulphur Springs, Warm Springs, Catoosa Springs and Thundering Springs in Georgia. These springs catered to "invalids" and proclaimed the medicinal qualities of their mineral waters, as well as their invigorating hot and cold thermal waters. However, a variety of social activities, hunting and fishing, mountain scenery, and, of course, escape from the hot and disease-ridden coastal plain, attracted the largest portion of the clientele. Social possibilities, entertainment offerings, physical facilities, and convenient access influenced selection.[55]

A somewhat mixed clientele patronized the two closest resorts in the foothills just north of Montgomery. Albert James Pickett, a very wealthy planter and one of Montgomery's leading citizens, maintained a summer house at Robinson Springs in the 1850s. He also visited springs that catered almost exclusively to the elite: Talladega Springs in 1857 and Bladon Springs the following year.[56]

In 1825 Huntsville's wealthy families popularized Blount Springs in north central Alabama. In the late 1820s and in the 1830s, the Cedar Hotel at Valhermoso Springs attracted guests from all over the Southeast, from the North and from Europe. However, it was Bladon Springs, which opened in 1838, that became antebellum Alabama's most famous watering place. Because of its proximity to Mobile and the Black Belt plantation country, it developed a quality clientele. At the height of the season as many as fifteen hundred visitors could be summering at Bladon Springs. Unlike most other mineral springs, it remained open year round so as to allow the sick to take its waters, which Mobile and New Orleans physicians recommended for their curative properties. Like other watering places, Bladon Springs offered more than mineral waters and bathing. The spa featured a skating rink, bowling alleys, billiards rooms and croquet grounds. Guests sat in the summer house built around the main spring, walked under the long pergola, flirted, played cards, danced in the ballroom in the evenings, and watched the children play on the grounds. The bar, in the hotel's raised basement, was open day and night. The opportunity for social interaction for members of the region's elite was a large part of the attraction. An endless round of non-productive activity and few responsibilities were not agreeable to everyone—even though such leisure unquestionably signified wealth. As several of the watering places had large tracts of land, hunting or fishing may have provided some relief.[57]

Montgomerians were not limited to summering at regional springs. Pensacola offered cooling sea breezes; the eastern shore of Mobile Bay offered sailing and Mobile society. More distant places, Lookout Mountain in Tennessee or mineral springs in Virginia, became possibilities as transportation improved. Lanier and Son, who managed Montgomery's finest hotel and one with its own mineral waters, also managed Montvale Springs. Montgomerians summered at Virginia's Rockbridge Alum Springs and Yellow Sulphur Springs; at two thousand feet, the latter touted its grand scenery and claimed to be Virginia's coolest summer resort. Perhaps as many as fifty thousand Southerners frequented Northern resorts each summer. Some Montgomerians probably visited Saratoga, New York, a particular favorite of Southerners until heightening political tensions made Southerners turn towards more friendly waters.[58]

Mineral springs, which began as resorts for invalids or as places to escape from the heat and disease of summer, took on a social function of great value for the wealthy. Of all the leisure activities of the antebellum period, summering at resorts did the most to establish and maintain the elite as a group apart. Those aspiring to be socially accepted could imitate the elite's choice of urban amusements; to an extent, they could even emulate the conspicuous consumption that the elite increasingly used to define itself and separate itself from the middling classes. But few could afford summering at resorts, because to do so required both wealth and discretionary time. Being together helped them develop a class consciousness; this was extremely significant for the elites of smaller cities who mixed with and perhaps adopted attitudes from those of the Northeastern cities where class lines had solidified by mid-century.[59]

Without question, the luxury of summering away from Montgomery separated the city's elite from all the rest. Although Montgomerians began summering at resorts in the mid-1820s, the importance of the institution increased as the wealth of individual families grew, as more families were able to leave the city in the summer, and especially as Montgomerians were able to go further afield. For Montgomerians, summering in the North helped break down provincialism and increased their class awareness. At the same time, summering in the North made Montgomerians even more aware of the peculiarities of their own culture.

How Montgomerians used their leisure time, while so similar to the North in many ways, points to deeper cultural differences. The attachment to certain aspects of what was believed to characterize aristocratic behavior or the Age of Chivalry—the South's peculiar form of romanticism—as well as the growth of Southern sectionalism at the end of the period manifested themselves in leisure activities—in tournaments, horse races, keeping open house, formal hospitality, exaggerated manners, and the military trappings for a variety of public activities.

3

Commercial Entertainment

In Montgomery's earliest years, gambling, excessive drinking, brawling and cockfighting dominated leisure choices. These continued throughout the antebellum period as attested by the reports of the mayor's court and efforts of the city council to control—but not eliminate—them. Members of all socioeconomic groups, including slaves, seem to have participated to one degree or another. Entertainment choices appeared very soon after Montgomery's founding. Horse racing meets, the first documented commercial entertainment, were followed by amateur theater, traveling troupes of professional actors and musicians, circuses and menageries, and minstrel shows. Professional, commercial entertainment transformed leisure time activities of nineteenth century towns and cities. Americans who patronized the increasing commercial entertainment offerings did so as audiences, spectators—not as participants as they had been in traditional or rural pastimes. Localities essentially lost control to regional or national commercial interests. Commercial entertainment, which varied little from region to region, helped homogenize the American public.

Montgomery's location near the Federal Road and near the head of navigation on the Alabama River ensured that traveling performers would visit the town. With variations, of course, the southern route for traveling troupes extended from Charleston and Savannah to Mobile and New Orleans; Augusta, Macon, Columbus and Montgomery were on the overland route. Most traveling theater companies that gave performances in Montgomery operated on circuits out of Mobile; late in the antebellum period Montgomery was included in the Georgia circuit. Although performances occurred throughout the year, few were given during the hottest months, when troupes tended to disband or work further north. Although no real "seasons" were established in Montgomery until the end of the antebellum period, the troupes generally gave performances from October through March. Montgomery's population increased during cooler months, and commercial entertainment promoters paid particular attention to audience potential. Throughout the antebellum period, Montgomery's small population threatened sustained commercial success.

Americans sought to determine whether or not commercial entertainment constituted appropriate use of leisure time, and if so, which types of commercial entertainment were acceptable. Many if not most churches opposed theaters, circuses and menageries, and minstrel shows. Many evangelical Christians viewed commercial entertainment, especially theater, as unproductive and frivolous, even evil. Some influential Montgomerians favored theatrical and operatic performances over circuses, menageries, and minstrel shows. However, in antebellum America and antebellum Montgomery the distinction between elite and popular entertainment had not yet been rigidly drawn, nor had the performing arts as highbrow culture been clearly separated from "mere" popular entertainment. Of course, the sophisticated and unsophisticated appreciated different aspects of the entertainment. These factors, and the lack of a first-rate theater building until the last few months of the period, made the success of professional theatrical entertainment in antebellum Montgomery tenuous.

Theater

The theater had a checkered history in antebellum Montgomery. Popular in the early 1830s, the theater did not thrive again until the end of the period, when regular theatrical seasons were established. Montgomery's theatrical history paralleled that of other inland cities as it evolved from amateur theatricals, to traveling stock or repertory companies, and finally to the star-system. Although a few Southerners wrote plays during the antebellum period—most notably in Charleston and New Orleans, the South's theater centers—the theater in the South was essentially indistinguishable from elsewhere in the country. The selections of plays and other amusements presented, the quality of acting, the behavior of the audience, and even the sophistication—or lack of it—did not differ from other cities, including those on the Atlantic Seaboard. In the age of the common man, the theater reflected American egalitarian ideals. Of course, society was stratified, but Americans, regardless of socioeconomic status or level of sophistication, experienced the theater together. Only at the end of the period, in the largest Eastern cities, did rigid spatial separation begin to occur.[1]

Montgomery's early theatrical offerings owed more to amateur efforts than professional ones. A group of young gentlemen organized the Thespian Society in the fall of 1822. They gave Montgomery's first recorded public performance, Shakespeare's *Julius Caesar*, on December 17, 1822. Many who were or who would become leading citizens were among the twenty-three amateur thespians acting in *Julius Caesar*, the main feature, and John O'Keeffe's *The Agreeable Surprise*, the "afterpiece." Benjamin Fitzpatrick played the title role, George W. B. Towns played Octavius Caesar, and Henry Goldthwaite played Mark Anthony. The three later played other leading roles: Fitzpatrick became governor of Alabama, a United States senator and president pro tempore of the Senate; Towns became governor of Georgia; and Goldthwaite became an associate justice of the Supreme Court of Alabama. The three read law under Judge Nimrod E. Benson, intendant of Montgomery, Master of the local Masonic lodge and later Grand Master of the Masonic Grand Lodge of Alabama. The three thespians were also Freemasons. These men represented Montgomery's interlocking leadership in its infancy.

In the spring of 1823, a visiting professional actor helped the Thespian Society put on several performances, including the Reverend Edward Young's *The Revenge*, an eighteenth century tragedy similiar to Shakespeare's *Othello*. Again leading citizens participated as actors, but no women are recorded as having played and probably none belonged to the Thespian Society. The young Daniel Sayre, later a newspaper editor, played Portia in *Julius Caesar*. Antebellum America's amateur theatrical groups helped develop public interest in dramatic performances and arranged venues for traveling professional troupes. Montgomery's Thespian Society was responsible for erecting a theater in 1829–30, but before that time the society had helped arrange professional performances.

Although *Julius Caesar* was the first recorded performance, other performances preceded it. Several of Montgomery earliest ordinances regulated plays and prohibited them on Sundays. In January 1820, Montgomery's town clerk granted a theatrical license to Moses Collier and Company, but nothing is known of this troupe's performances.

Considering the great difficulty of travel before the coming of the railroads, it is surprising that any traveling troupes appeared in Montgomery. But they came, on foot and horseback, in stages and barouches, with light spring wagons and heavy road wagons, and on flat-bottomed boats and steamboats. In January 1824, the Vaughan Family Troupe presented *The Microcosm*, a moral lecture ridiculing worldly behavior that was enlivened by serious and comic songs. The Vaughans had presented the same performance in Boston, New York, New Orleans and St. Louis.[2]

The first major professional stock company to perform in Montgomery was Noah Miller Ludlow's, which played for two weeks in mid-December 1827. The venue arranged by the Thespian Society was rather primitive.

> The room that we performed in at Montgomery was, perhaps, the most inconvenient place that ever the descendants of Thespis had to encounter. It was in the upper story of a very large, roughly built frame house, that was called a "hotel;" the garret, or topmost portion of which had been fitted up by some amateurs to perform plays in. The only way of reaching this attic temple of the muses, for either actors or audience, was by a flight of rough stairs on the *outside* of the building, and these seemed almost interminable; then, when you had reached the top of them, you had to make your entrance through a *window*, so low that a person of ordinary height had to stoop to get into the room. This room was fitted up with rough seats without any covering, and all on a dead level. There were no dressing-rooms contiguous to the stage; therefore the performers were compelled to dress in their own rooms on the stories below, and, wrapped in cloaks, thread their way among the audience to the stage. If a change of dress was required during the progress of a play, it had to be done behind a temporary screen across one corner of the room, and behind the back scene. I was told the room had been fitted up for some amateur actors of the town . . .[3]

For more than a year, no other professional stock companies came to Montgomery. In 1829 Ludlow's company made a second appearance, but only after a fire destroyed the company's theater in Mobile. Beginning in mid-March 1829 they played for several weeks while a new Mobile theater was being prepared. Ludlow's was the largest and best company to play in Montgomery during the early years, and Montgomery audiences were probably very appreciative. Ludlow recognized that the town's small population could not support his large company, although he was glad to meet expenses.

Sol Smith's company was invited to come to Montgomery from Tuscaloosa, then the state capital, and to open the Thespian Society's newly-built, attractive, but still unfinished, theater. The company opened for a two-week run in late January 1830. Madame Anna Feron, the great opera soprano, appeared with Smith's troupe for the first two nights of the successful run. The opening of the theater seems to have stimulated the Thespian Society and the audience. In March and September 1830, and again in July 1831, the amateurs gave productions, but then did not perform again until 1835. Sol Smith returned to Montgomery with a new company in March 1832. He returned rather frequently until his last performance in Montgomery in July 1835. Although the weather was extremely hot, his admirers filled the house to capacity. Montgomery audiences had appreciated Sol Smith, and he them. In 1843 Smith and Ludlow formed a partnership, and until 1853 the two dominated the New Orleans-Mobile-St. Louis theatrical circuit. Although they played Mobile in the winter, they did not return to Montgomery.[4]

Audiences of the time, including major Eastern cities, openly expressed their approval or disapproval, even forcing actors to alter their performances on the spot. On one occasion in Montgomery, the audience demanded that an actor, who had just concluded an extremely serious scene in Delpini's *Don Juan*, in which he played a statue of the murdered governor, interrupt the performance and entertain them with a comic dance. Apparently they had enjoyed his comic dances previously and saw no incongruity in his performing one just after the tragic climax of *Don Juan*. The actor protested, but Sol Smith urged him to oblige the audience, which he did. Smith recorded that "the audience relished the dance hugely; and I must say that the marble statue, dancing to the tune of 'A frog he would a-wooing go,' *was* a most original and mirth-provoking affair."[5] Antebellum audiences throughout the country exhibited a similar lack of decorum. Diasappointed audiences typically booed and pelted actors. Delighted audiences shouted, stomped their feet, and possibly demanded that a scene, speech, song or dance be repeated. Audience members overly engaged in the story occasionally shouted warnings or threats, or even intervened physically; spectators frequently sang along with the actors. Theatergoers routinely talked and visited; men smoked cigars, drank liquor, and ate—the cracking of hard-shelled nuts was particularly loud and annoying. Prostitutes confined to the upper gallery tried to attract customers; some actually practiced their profession on the premises. Theatergoers themselves did not widely condemn rowdy behavior, although it shocked English visitors and deterred most ladies from frequenting the theaters.[6]

Public opinion was divided about the theater's influence on society. Sol Smith, who had influential supporters in Montgomery, took offense to criticism that the theater was too exciting and too expensive, that it was surrounded by incidental evils, and that it led young men to become immoral and dissipated. Sophisticated theater supporters not only enjoyed dramatic performances, but also believed that drama benefited society by portraying the consequences of both moral and immoral behavior and by providing a safety valve for venting emotions that could be destructive if vented elsewhere.[7]

Controversy, of course, affected the rising and falling fortunes of professional theatrical companies. In a town with a potential audience as small as Montgomery's, public acceptance of the theater was crucial. An October 1825 editorial-review in the *Alabama Journal* stated that some in the community believed that the theater would "estrange the youthful mind from the paths of virtue."[8] But a subsequent letter to the editor recommended George Lillo's tragedy *George Barnwell* to fathers and masters.

> We are those who consider the stage, under judicious management, as the most salutary school for morals, and the most effectual refiner of the manners, that a community can support; for it unites . . . example with

precept—and enforces, or rather impresses, all its maxims on the mind under the enticing garb of pleasure.[9]

Throughout the country, churches led the opposition to the theater; opposition was strongest in New England. In 1829 and 1831, Montgomery's Methodists tried to buy the Thespian Society's new theater to use it for their meeting house and, probably, to confound attempts to continue theatrical presentations. The conflict became so heated by March 1832 that the theater's supporters were prepared to buy the land out from under the existing, dilapidated Methodist Church building. The theater's affluent supporters almost succeeded in buying the lot, before General John Scott, whose wife was a Methodist, arrived at the eleventh hour, bid five hundred dollars, and ended the auction. Soon afterwards, General Scott gave the land to the Methodist Church.[10]

Sol Smith related another example of opposition to the theater. The large size of both Smith's company and Montgomery's theater made it financially difficult to sustain a lengthy season. Consequently, the company would occasionally play in outlying towns. In 1835 they played for two weeks in a billiard room in Wetumpka, which Smith called "that remarkably primitive city," and in an academy room in Hayneville.

> For twelve successive nights we exerted ourselves for their edification, and to this day I am in utter ignorance whether our efforts were satisfactory or not, for not a hand of applause greeted us during the whole time, neither did a smile—a laugh was out of the question—shed its ray, to cheer us on in our task.[11]

One man in the audience began to laugh during a performance of Isaac Bickerstaff's comedy *The Hypocrite*, only to be cut short by an elder of the Presbyterian Church, who ordered the man to quit laughing or leave the room.[12]

In early 1840 Montgomery's Baptist Church conference unanimously adopted a strict resolution regarding public amusements.

> Believing it to be inconsistent with a profession of religion and contrary to the doctrines and principles of the gospel to attend places of public amusement and of doubtful character, such as the theatre, circus, and such like places, and whereas the gospel enjoins on those who profess its principles to depart from all iniquity and the least appearance of evil. Therefore, Resolved, that the church will in the future deem any member participating in such activities guilty of immoral conduct and liable to the censure of the church.[13]

Although unanimously adopted by the church conference, it may not have been universally accepted by all members of the congregation. The resolution regarding the theater—and the minister's support of the Whigs in the election of 1840, his wife's family's support of abolition, and the failure of the church to pay the minister—contributed to his resignation in January 1842.[14]

An editorial in 1860 summed up the unresolved debate over the propriety of the theater. Some saw "sin and Satan" in the theater, especially people who had never attended the performances, but the editor maintained that "the stage was originally intended to correct the manners, improve the taste, and virtually to inculcate the principles of morality under the garb of pleasure."[15] Considering the offerings, however, the theater probably entertained more than it edified the audience.

Public support of the theater waned after Sol Smith's company left in July 1835; the occasional performances that occurred were apparently not well attended. The Panic of 1837 adversely affected entertainment troupes throughout the country. In 1839, W. R. Hart attempted to rebuild support for the Montgomery theater by emphasizing drama's instructive nature, but the religious revival in the fall of 1839 hampered his endeavors. The Thespian Society was reformed in 1843, this time with amateurs and professionals performing together. Although they conducted themselves so as to bring no criticism on the theater, nothing lasting seems to have come of their efforts. The religious revival that began in the summer of 1845 and lasted for three months must have turned Montgomerians away from the theater.[16]

In February 1849, W. R. Hart again attempted to gather support for the professional theater. The editor of the *Alabama Journal*, always a supporter of the theater, welcomed its return. Hart fitted up the saloon or formal reception room of the Exchange Hotel, the city's finest, as his theater. Unfortunately for Hart's troupe, a minstrel show and a menagerie presented fierce competition. Attendance for Hart's *Romeo and Juliet* suffered somewhat, but his season overall was satisfactory. Such failures to coordinate performance schedules and venues caused confusion and divided the potential audience.[17]

The 1840s were not a good decade for theater in Montgomery, yet the situation was not better elsewhere. Ludlow, who had had very bad years in 1842, 1844 and 1845 in St. Louis, New Orleans and Mobile attributed the dramatic drop off in audiences to the money crisis. Harry Watkins, playwright, actor, and impresario who worked all over the eastern half of the country in the last two decades of the antebellum period, attributed poor audiences to the vagaries of a one-crop economy (in the South) and to competition or the weather (in the North). Actually, theatrical companies always risked financial failure.

The first half of the 1850s was also a lean time for the theater in Montgomery. A combination of factors confounded attempts to revive the theater. The extremely cold winter of 1852, the stormy spring of 1853, and the drought of 1855, made travel difficult and injured Montgomery's economy. Smallpox struck in 1851, and severe outbreak of yellow fever occurred in 1853 and 1854. Many fled the city, and others, believing the fevers to be contagious, simply stayed away—theatrical troupes proved unwilling to expose themselves. The tense national political situation diminished interest in theatrical diversions, and moral opposition to the theater persisted. Finally, the city lacked a modern theater building. Nevertheless, had a large supportive audience existed in Montgomery, the theater probably could have flourished amid the adverse conditions of the early 1850s.

Newspaper editors consistently promoted the theater and downplayed other amusements. In January 1853, William H. Crisp, an Irishman who relocated to Georgia and became a regional theatrical manager, visited Montgomery to assess support for construction of a large, elegant theater. Although he did not undertake a new theater building, he did attempt to revive theatrical productions.[18] In February 1853, the *Alabama Journal*

Newspaper advertisement for Crisp and Canning's attempts to hold the public's attention. Montgomery Daily Advertiser, December 13, 1859.

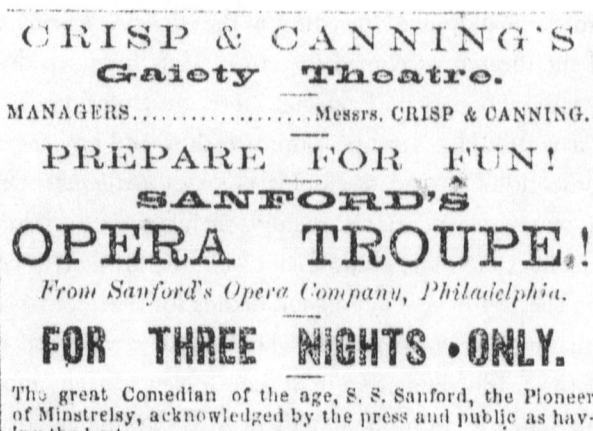

praised Crisp's *Macbeth* and encouraged every young man in the community to attend Edward Moore's tragedy *The Gamester* to "witness this exhibition of the terrible, evil effects and pernicious influences of the detestable vice of gambling—which are drawn so graphically in this play."[19]

The economic boom of the last half of the 1850s spurred major construction in the city; public services expanded, institutions strengthened, and Montgomery finally seemed ready to embrace the theater. Poor performances, the lack of a modern playhouse, and competition from minstrel shows, however, marred most seasons. In 1857, the Ward Theatrical Company set up Commercial Hall—with two large anterooms, seating for a thousand, good ventilation, and excellent acoustics—as a playhouse. With an adequate venue available, the Duffield Company arrived in October 1857 with "stars" in addition to the twenty or thirty members of the stock company. Duffield mounted a program of plays to appeal to a variety of tastes. The company attended to details—such as makeup—and reduced admission fees, only to again fall victim to the greater appeal of the visiting Campbell

Minstrels. Because of the failures of 1857, only one theatrical troupe appeared in Montgomery in 1858. Despite new scenery and costumes and a good selection of plays, it could not succeed against the Campbell Minstrels playing at Concert Hall. William Crisp, undaunted, tried again in January and February 1859. With a full company, orchestra, and singing and dancing, he succeeded. He intended to return in the fall, but his plans changed, and the city was deprived of a fall theatrical season.[20]

Meanwhile, construction of a new theater building was underway. Its auditorium had about nine hundred seats, all with unobstructed sightlines. The *Weekly Post* praised the new theater with the customary hyperbole.

> For style, beauty, and convenience of arrangement this theatre has no superior and but few equals in any Southern city. The size is amply sufficient for a Montgomery audience; the architecture of the latest and most approved style, and the paintings and ornamental work most brilliant and exquisitely beautiful.[21]

The new Montgomery Theatre allowed for spatial separation of the audience based on ticket price. Apparently the old theater and the other venues had not rigidly separated socioeconomic groups; generally there had been only two admission prices—full and half, the latter for children and blacks. The new theater's auditorium was probably constructed in the manner common for most antebellum theaters of any size: boxes for couples, ladies and the wealthy clientele; the pit (orchestra) and first balcony for single men and less affluent whites; and the upper balcony for blacks and prostitutes. For all the egalitarian talk, antebellum theatergoers, especially in the final decade of the period, used spatial separation to divide socioeconomic groups.[22]

Newspaper advertisements for the opening of the new theater appeared as early as September 1860. Actors and actresses with significant previous performances were listed: Edwin Booth, John Wilkes [Booth], Daniel and Emma Waller, and Maggie Mitchell. The Booth brothers were natives of Maryland; Edwin was already a well-established actor, having played in New York and distant California, and John Wilkes Booth was just beginning his meteoric career. Daniel Waller of New York and his English wife Emma had played in England, the United States, and Australia; she was one of the major emotive actresses of the American theater. Margaret, or Maggie, Mitchell was a New Yorker who had first gone on the stage at twelve; after the Civil War she became a leading American actress. The advertisement also announced that a "full orchestra" under Professor Herman Frank Arnold would accompany the performances. To deflect criticism on moral grounds and to shame those who preferred the minstrels, promoters advertised the theater as "intellectual entertainment."[23]

The Montgomery Theatre opened October 22, 1860, with an address, a dramatic rendition of the National Anthem by the entire company, Richard Brinsley Sheridan's *School for Scandal* as the main feature, and a farce as the afterpiece. Just eight hundred attended. The reviewer in the *Montgomery Weekly Post* cited the conflict with the Firemen's Ball and lamented the less than full house, but asserted, "This Company, altogether, we hesitate not to say, is not only the most brilliant that has ever appeared before a Montgomery audience, but fully equal to any theatrical Corps in any Southern city."[24]

Reviews in the *Montgomery Weekly Post* and *Montgomery Weekly Advertiser* for the remainder of the season were glowing rhetorical accounts of fine performances that were well received by the audiences. When audiences were small, the reviewers expressed regret, usually offering excuses. The reviewers for the *Advertiser* and the *Post* seem to have gone to every performance, liked them all, and especially appreciated Maggie Mitchell. Their interest in Mitchell was not at all unusual, as many theatergoers then, as now, were as much interested in the actors and actresses as in the plays. Theatrical companies, of course, realized this and advertised their stars. Actresses were particularly appreciated in the South; they were believed to be romantic, certainly not on pillars to be worshipped in the way that Southern gentlemen supposedly worshipped their mothers, sweethearts and wives. The *Post's* reviewer also mentioned John Wilkes Booth, who was enthusiastically received in his first appearance on the Montgomery stage in R. L. Shiel's tragedy *The Apostate* in which he played Pescara, the villain. Booth also played in the title roles in *Richard III* and in *Rafaelle*. The last theatrical season of the antebellum period exceeded all the rest.[25]

The plays performed in Montgomery were identical to those performed elsewhere in the country, with the exceptions of *Othello* and *Uncle Tom's Cabin*. The former was performed and accepted in the South as an antimiscegenation lesson until late in the period when performances ceased. Parodies of *Uncle Tom's Cabin* were also performed in the South from 1853 to 1855 and then revived in 1860–61. Theatrical companies did not adapt to conform to local taste; they presented in Montgomery what was the fashion in New York, and, except for American plays, the fashion of New York followed that of London.

Tragedies or comedies, as opposed to farces, were generally an evening's main feature. Comedies were featured twice as often as tragedies. Shakespeare's tragedies and comedies, not his history plays (with the major exception of *Richard III*), were frequently performed, usually in rewritten versions adapted to the antebellum preference for melodrama's clear-cut distinction between good and evil. Shakespearean productions helped legitimize the theater in the eyes of its critics, and individual stars made names for themselves in certain Shakespearean roles. Furthermore, Shakespearean plays were as well suited to diverse antebellum audiences as they had been to diverse Elizabethan audiences; they offered melodrama, oratory and violence to the unsophisticated, and the beauty of English language to the sophisticated. Shakespearean adaptations, however, lost subtlety of characterization and intricacy of plot. Aside from Shakespeare, many eighteenth-century British plays and contemporary British and American plays served in the repertoires; audiences preferred the sentimental and melodramatic.

Farces usually preceded and almost always followed the main feature. An evening's entertainment also could include pantomimes, tableaux, dances and music, predominantly sentimental or comic. Variety best ensured that all patrons were satisfied. If any group was neglected, it was likely to be the sophisticated, since theatrical companies were commercial undertakings that had to please the masses to survive.

Except for not building a first-class playhouse until the end of the period, Montgomery's theatrical history followed the norm of antebellum America. The theater flourished briefly in the early years, when competition from other commercial entertainment was limited and small traveling theatrical stock companies mounted only short runs. The later emergence of larger companies and the star system increased costs. Moral opposition to the theater, economic downturns, and a variety of other influences prevented the duplication of the theater's early successes. The potential audience was too small for the theater to compete successfully against the more popular minstrels and circuses. The theater in Montgomery, as elsewhere in the United States, attempted to cater to everyone: the elite, the respectable classes, mechanics and prostitutes, and when they had the price of admission, laborers and blacks. The defense of the theater as a temple of art and culture and a means for moral uplift notwithstanding, theatergoers went to the theater to enjoy themselves. For most patrons, the theater was not art whose purpose was to entertain and instruct; it was merely entertainment.[26]

Opera

The distinction that now exists between popular and classical or cultivated music was not finely drawn in antebellum America. Essentially the same audience attended and appreciated a variety of performances. Montgomerians applauded a boy drummer, fifer, banjo player, bagpiper, ballad singer and minstrels, as well as violinists, pianists and symphonic groups. Furthermore, individual performers presented varied programs to appeal to many tastes and as large an audience as possible. American audiences outside the major urban areas could not be too discriminating because performers appeared infrequently. Not all antebellum America's major stars and troupes performed in Montgomery. Several parties of Montgomerians went to New Orleans and Mobile in 1851 to hear Jenny Lind, the Swedish Nightingale. Montgomerians also went to Mobile to see Charlotte Cushman, the famous actress and singer.[27]

Touring opera singers performed as individual stars, in full Italian and English operas, and in operatic burlesques. All of these operatic forms were presented to Montgomery audiences. Elizabeth Feron, the English soprano who first came to the United States in 1828, sang for the January 1830 opening of the old Montgomery Theatre.

> Madame Feron, the great singer, performed with us two nights, and as we were without a regular orchestra, various means were resorted to for

an accompaniment to her songs. A piano-forte was introduced upon the stage, and she accompanied herself in some pieces—in others she pressed me into the service... the beautiful song, "As I hang on your bosom," was gloriously breathed forth by the great prima donna of European Opera, in a theatre surrounded by uncut trees, and occupied by an audience whose appreciation was as warm as that of the dilettanti of Italy.

Madame Feron entered into the spirit of the scene, and seemed to enjoy herself very much, imparting her good humor to all around, both before and behind the curtain.[28]

That an opera star of Feron's renown appeared at such an early date in a town such as Montgomery and with a theatrical troupe may have been unusual. There was no doubt, however, that she was the main attraction, as she received a disproportionate amount of the box office receipts.

Other opera stars appeared in Montgomery. In March 1848 and again in June 1850, the English soprano Anna Reviere Bishop appeared. Her 1848 Southern tour also included Charleston, Savannah, Mobile and New Orleans. Her troupe was not as large as it was when it played in Boston, New York and Philadelphia, but it did include the bass William Brough, a secondary English star. If their Montgomery performances were like those elsewhere on the Southern tour, they would have sung in both English and Italian and would have been well received by large audiences.[29]

In the first week of April 1849, the Van Deussen minstrels played opposite the Leati Operatic Group. The Montgomery audience, however, preferred Van Duessen's blind minstrels at Montgomery Hall to the Leati opera concert in the saloon of the Exchange Hotel. The editor of the *Alabama Journal* was not amused that the city preferred minstrels to the high art of the Leatis. The opera group was persuaded to give another performance, it was well attended, and the city's honor was redeemed. The Leatis, who probably sang in English, were followed by an Italian opera company. In February 1855, Madame Rosa de Vries and her opera troupe presented selections from several operas. All of these early opera performances were operatic selections, rather than full operas.

In the spring of 1858, however, Montgomery had a genuine opera season, its only one during the antebellum period. The New Orleans English Opera Company performed for two weeks in March. Its repertory was typical of other English companies, and with two exceptions, the identical repertory was presented in Charleston that year. In Montgomery, the company performed *La Sonnambula, Barber of Seville, The Bohemian Girl, Fra Diavolo, Daughter of the Regiment, Crown Diamonds* and *Il Trovatore*. Vincenzo Bellini's *La Sonnambula*, with its simple story and opportunities for vocal display, was among the most popular operas of nineteenth century America. Only the last opera, translated into English and usually known as *The Troubador*, was an attempt to keep up with newer Italian operas. The New Orleans English Opera Company toured widely in the South and West from 1857 to 1859. But, as it did not perform in Boston or New York, the New Orleans English Opera Company was ignored by the Eastern musical press. The two-week Montgomery run was financially unsuccessful. This can probably be attributed to the company primarily being composed of stock-company singing actors. There were no stars, and audiences attended

Operatic panic from La Somnambula, *as depicted in* Harper's Weekly *for December 22, 1860.*

to see stars more than to see the performance.

For a week in mid-December 1858, the Buckley Opera Troupe performed for appreciative Montgomery audiences. Unlike the spring opera season, the Christmas season was profitable. The troupe was actually a group of serenaders and Ethiopian burlesquers, rather than a formal opera company. Their burlesque performances of *Lucretia Borgia* and *La Somnambula* were highly appreciated. Operatic burlesques left the music basically intact, but substituted humorous or ridiculous lyrics and dramatic situations. The humor often hinged on blatantly racist lyrics and exaggerated black dialect. Operatic burlesques, however, were not merely amusements for the unsophisticated. In New York, where the parodies began in the late 1830s, the audiences for operatic burlesque and for Italian opera were likely to have been very similar, because to enjoy the burlesques completely patrons had to be familiar with the operas or at least the operatic music being parodied. Although the Montgomery audience was not very familiar with opera performances, they were familiar with operatic music. Operatic music was presented in the theater as part of dramatic performances; it was played and sung in homes; it was used for dance music, for brass bands, and even for organ grinders. More directly, Montgomerians heard operatic music performed by virtuoso instrumentalist Henri Vieuxtemps and Sigismund Thalberg, the great Norwegian violinist Ole Bull, and the renowned soprano Mariette Piccolomini and contralto Amalia Patti.

These performers, however, did not present exclusively sophisticated programs. Patti sang some popular songs—"Home Sweet Home" and "Comin' thro' the Rye"—and was loudly applauded. Bull played "Katy Darling," "Arkansas Traveler," "Pop Goes the Weasel" and "Last Rose of Summer," as well as the grand aria from *Puritani* and selections from *La Sonnambula*. The Montgomery audience, therefore, had the opportunity to hear both popular and operatic music.[30]

Montgomery's opera audiences probably were cross-sections of the community, but less so than the theater and certainly not as representative of the general population as the audiences of minstrel shows and circuses. Many, such as laborers whose daily wages were approximately one dollar, were deterred or excluded by ticket prices. For example, the Parodi Italian

Opera Company that performed *La Sonnambula* in early April 1860 asked one dollar fifty cents for reserved seats and one dollar for unreserved ones, and the libretto in English and Italian further increased the cost. Although antebellum opera was not a form of entertainment reserved for the elite, it must have had a greater appeal for the sophisticated. Nevertheless, it was entertainment appreciated by members of all strata of society, such as television or films are today. Frederick Law Olmsted, who was convinced that blacks had some innate gift for music, wrote that he had been told that slaves could be heard whistling opera tunes quite accurately the day after a performance.

During the antebellum period, elites of large Northeastern cities failed in their attempts to change a popular entertainment into an exclusive art form. Even in New York, the elite was not numerous enough to support Italian opera without middling and working class help. In New York the general public resented attempts to exclude them from operatic performances, and a backlash developed, especially against Italian opera. As Italian opera was foreign and as it was associated with the elite, public patronage did fall off somewhat. English opera capitalized on being "opera for the people." Nevertheless, the same Italian and English opera companies that performed in the large East Coast cities, traveled the country performing for audiences of all but the lowest stratum of society.[31] They were appreciated in Montgomery as they were appreciated elsewhere.

CIRCUSES AND MENAGERIES

Circuses and menageries provided the most exciting, exotic and popular entertainment in antebellum Montgomery. In January 1829, an equestrian act traveling by the steamboat *Amazon* demonstrated feats of horsemanship and put on a fireworks display to the satisfaction of the audience. The first real circus did not occur until December 1831. For five days, Yeaman's Circus presented gymnastic and equestrian acts. Over the next twenty-nine years, more than twenty-five circuses and menageries exhibited in Montgomery. Beginning in 1849, a year of six circuses and menageries, exhibitions visited more frequently. Circuses and menageries, like other forms of amusement, tended to occur from October through March, although at least three circuses were mounted in the summer.

Before 1851 when the menagerie was added to the circus arena show, circuses and menageries exhibited separately. This arrangement was more profitable; had they exhibited together, the public would have expected both for the price of one. When menageries and circuses traveled together, such as the Waring and Raymond's Circus and Menagerie that had a three-day stand in February 1839, the public viewed the menagerie during the day and the circus at night. Furthermore, as circuses were merely entertainment, and immoral in the eyes of some, Sunday performances were ruled out. Menageries, advertised as educational, could be exhibited in some places on Sundays. To bill exhibits as educational or as displays of the diversity of God's creation deflected criticism and attracted patrons who were increasingly interested in the natural sciences.[32]

In December 1840, J. Clayton exhibited a giraffe, or "cameleopard," which he advertised as being the first in the United States. His large advertisement in the *Alabama Journal* featured a picture of two giraffes and stated that two hundred fifty thousand had seen the exhibit in the preceding eight months. The advertisement also claimed that the exhibit was displayed with "chastity, morality and virtue," and that it was for "the old, the young, the grave, the gay, the moral, religious, intellectual and refined." To improve the tone of his exhibition still further Clayton built a large pavilion with elevated and carpeted seats and, for those wanting to attend for scientific and educational purposes only, provided a ten to one o'clock showing. Although these patrons would not have to attend in the circus-like atmosphere of the evening, they were charged the full admission—one dollar.[33]

Exhibitors advertised unfamiliar animals or animals not native to the United States as "animal curiosities." The first lion was exhibited in America in 1716 and the first elephant in 1796, but the first giraffe was not exhibited until 1837 nor a gorilla until 1850. Thus ordinary people and amateur scientists alike considered them curiosities. The interest displayed by amateur scientists, many of whom were physicians, legitimized the curiosity of the general public. The controversy and publicity that came from questions of the authenticity of some animal or human exhibitions merely served to increase attendance.[34]

Spectacle, not curiosity and educational possibilities, really drew the crowds. In January 1851, Welch and Nathan's National Circus entered Montgomery in a parade led by the "Grande Armanxa" pulled by thirty horses; this "Imperial Chariot" was the bandwagon for the New York Knickerbocker Brass Band. The bandwagon illustrates that the circus was being transformed from equestrian and gymnastic acts to grand spectacle: the wagon was advertised as having been modeled on the imperial chariot of Cyrus the Great, with gold and silver decorative eagles, equestrians, and stars and flowers in the style of Louis XIV.[35] The circus itself included acrobatic performances, equestrian acts, comic routines, singing and dancing, an impersonation of a "Wild Indian of the Desert," and even banjo players and "delineators of Negro characters."[36]

Johnson and Company's People's Circus appeared in April 1851. Each performance was in the evening; admission was fifty cents for free adults and twenty-five cents for children and blacks—standard admission fees for the period. The circus featured equestrian and acrobatic events, and clowns, including John May, "scholar, wit, orator and jester" and Ben Jennings, "humorist, stump speaker, punster and essence of drollery."[37]

Gilbert R. Spaulding's and Charles J. Rogers's Circus and Floating Palace, accompanied by Raymond's Menagerie or the North American Circus, appeared in January 1853, December 1854, and again in February 1855. These circuses were the most spectacular to visit antebellum Montgomery. Bandwagons pulled by many horses or by several elephants generally led circus parades. However, the excited crowds and the movements of wagons and animals drowned out the sound of the bands. Dr. Spaulding invented a large bandwagon, the "Apollonicon," dedicated to the "Spirit of '76"; it produced the music of organ pipes, whistles, reeds, horns, drums, triangles, gongs and cymbals. Forty horses, four abreast, pulled the Apollonicon.

The expense and time lost to move a very large circus over the poor roads of the times led Spaulding to move his circus and the Apollonicon by a large barge, towed by two light-draft boats. Such an arrangement reduced logistical problems of transportation, of housing performers and animals, and of setting up and breaking down the exhibits and the enclosed arena. The barge, which cost forty-two thousand dollars, had a forty-two foot ring

COMMERCIAL ENTERTAINMENT 85

This sketch of Spalding & Rogers's Floating Palace appeared in Gleason's Pictorial Drawing-Room Companion, *February 19, 1853.*

in its center. Mirrors on either side gave the illusion of multiple rings. The cream and gold Floating Palace decorated with carvings, paintings, mirrors, carpeting and draperies and lit by gas lights was more elaborate than the finest venue in any but the largest cities. The barge seated two thousand four hundred in a roofed amphitheater: a dress circle of a thousand cane-bottom chairs, a family circle of five hundred cushioned "settees," and a nine-hundred seat gallery. Interest expressed by Mobile convinced the owners to tow the Floating Palace to Mobile from the Mississippi where it had been operating. From Mobile successful tours were made on the Tombigbee and Alabama rivers. Enormous crowds greeted the Floating Palace in Mobile and Montgomery. The circus announced its coming with the "Apollonicon" and its arrival with a cannon. Patrons viewed the accompanying menagerie, displayed on one of the towboats, as they moved along the wharf to the circus which was held in the Floating Palace itself.[38]

The February 1856, entrance of the combined Mabie's Menagerie and Den Stone's Circus and Tyler's Indian Exhibition vied with the spectacle of

*Opposite Page: Newspaper advertisements for Mabie's Menagerie, Den Stone's Circus, and Tyler's Indian Exhibition (*Montgomery Advertiser, *February 13, 1856) and Crescent City Circus (*Montgomery Advertiser and State Gazette, *May 14, 1856).*

the Apollonicon and Floating Palace. Five elephants pulling the music chariot with its full band led the procession. The equestrian company, "brilliantly mounted on their highly trained horses," and the "chiefs, braves and sages of the Seneca Indian tribe" followed. The "caravan of wild beasts drawn in their cages" brought up the rear. The circus itself included equestrian and acrobatic acts and a lion tamer who exhibited "his astonishing control over the wild beasts in the den of lions." The Indian exhibition consisted of a series of scenes illustrating "savage life"—a buffalo hunt, corn gathering, "grotesque dancing," bird and thanksgiving dances, and Seneca war songs and whooping.[39]

The combined Van Amburgh and Company's and Broadway menageries exhibited in March 1859 and in January 1860 as Van Amburgh's Zoological Show and Circus. Billed as "the only moral and instructive Exhibit in America," the exhibitions featured "beasts, birds and reptiles from the four quarters of the globe; among which may be found Hannibal, the mammoth Elephant of the World, weighing nearly 15,000 lbs. The only pairs of African Ostriches in America—nine feet high!" Also being exhibited was a black alpaca sheep, a lioness, and a "sacred cow."[40] When Isaac A. Van Amburgh first appeared in Montgomery, he had been exhibiting his menageries for a quarter of a century. In 1838 he had toured in England, where he eventually owned the largest wagon show in that country. His menageries got a great boost of respectability when Queen Victoria watched six shows in six weeks, observed the animals being fed and talked with Van Amburgh himself.

The popularity of wild animal exhibits was directly connected with the fear that the animals raised in the audience—not the so-called moral or educational value of the exhibitions. Hannibal, one of the largest elephants in the United States, was advertised as having killed seven people. To increase the ferocity of his lions, Van Amburgh was accused of starving them

MABIE'S MENAGERIE, DEN STONE'S CIRCUS, AND TYLER'S INDIAN EXHIBITION!
COMBINED!

THE object of the proprietors in combining in one immense show three distinct and perfect exhibitions, at a single price of admission, is to place within the means of all an opportunity of witnessing these magnificent wonders of art and nature.

The following distinguished members of the Equestrian profession, are comprised in the troupe of DEN STONE:

W. W. NICHOLS,   J. DEMOTT,   D. ROGERS,
E. W. PERRY,   O. DODGE,   MAST. CARPENTER,
G. DEMOTT,   E. STONE,   MAST. LEON.
Clown..................................DEN STONE.

Will exhibit at MONTGOMERY
Friday and Saturday, February 15 and 16,
☞ FOR TWO DAYS ONLY. ☜
☞ Doors open on Friday at 6½ o'clock, P. M.—on Saturday at 2 and 6½ o'clock, P. M.
Admission 50 cents—Children and servants 25 cents.

THE GRAND PROCESSION!
Of the Three Troupes will enter town in the forenoon, in the following order:
THE SUPERB MUSIC CHARIOT!
WITH FULL BAND—DRAWN BY FIVE ELEPHANTS!
EQUESTRIAN COMPANY!
Brilliantly mounted on their highly trained horses. The Chiefs, Braves and Sages of the
Seneca Indian Tribe!
Caravan of Wild Beasts!
Drawn in their Cages.

The Scenes in the Ring will embrace every variety of
Horsemanship, Vaulting, Tumbling,
SOMERSETTING, ACROBATIC FEATS, &c.

MR. BEASLEY
Will exhibit his astonishing control over the Wild Beasts,
IN THE DEN OF LIONS!

Foremost among the attractive novelties of this Company, are the characteristic performances of the
WILD TENANTS OF THE FOREST!
Illustrating scenes of savage life.
BUFFALO HUNT!
And again, in an amusing Pastoral Scene, called
THE CORN GATHERING!
Interspersed with Grotesque Dancing, Singing, Whooping, &c.; besides the following:
The Bird Dance—Thanksgiving Dance!
War Song of the Senecas, &c.
☞ For further particulars, see Pictorials, (large and small) Descriptive Bills, Lithographs, &c., of the Company.
feb7–td

CRESCENT CITY CIRCUS.

One Hundred and Twenty Men and Horses.
GRANDEST PROCESSION OF THE AGE!
NO HUMBUG, NO INDIANS, NO ANIMALS.
A GOOD OLD FASHIONED CIRCUS!
Such as used to Travel Thirty Years Ago.
WM. C. MANAHAN,
SOLE PROPRIETOR.

Mr. JOHN SHEAY, Sr .... EQUESTRIAL DIRECTOR.
Mr. WILLIAM MIDDLETON .... TREASURER.

☞ Admission 50 cents—Children and servants 25 cents.
Doors open at 1 and 6—Performance to commence at 2 and 7.

WILL EXHIBIT AT
Montgomery.................May 28, 29 and 30.
Talladega....................May 21 and 22.
Syllacogga...................May 23.
Bradford's....................May 24.
Wetumpka...................May 26 and 27.

SIX GREAT CLOWNS!
JIMMEY REYNOLDS,
The Orator of the Ring as the Least.
Immense Feats of
AQUESTRIANISM STRENGTH AND ELEGANCE.
Only one Star in the firmament shining more brightly, appearing more beautiful than "Venus rising from the sea,"
M'lle. Franck Vic.
The Floral Equestrienne,
Who introduces her Troup of Elfin Ponies—so small as to be wonders in nature, so graceful as to claim universal admiration, so novel in performance as to surprise all beholders!!!

MADAME SHOWLES,
The English Lady delineator of the scenes of Tournament and Chivalry, will represent the Queen of "LOVE AND BEAUTY" as in the days of Ivanhoe, and Ashby de la Zouche.

MAD'LLE FRANCK VIC,
Changing from her gentle introduction of the Miniature Steeds, so elegantly pleasing, will excite the astonishment and even fear, of the audience, by performing the wild, unruly, and fierce Mexican Pet Horse,
EUREKA,
and show that careful training can cause the Fiery steed of the Desert to become submissive and obedient to a beautiful and innocent girl.

THE BANDS.
In addition to the Fine Brass Band which accompanies the Troupe, another Band of a purely novel character leads its sweet sounds to the General Minstrelsy—a Band of Harps.

"SWEET AS THOSE OF TARA'S HALLS."

GREAT EQUESTRIANS
W..............................accomplished
Mr. O. DALE,
the renowned graceful Rider, and One Hundred somersaults. His great achievements make him the favorite of the Ring

Mr. W. D. SMITH,
A Six Horse Rider of such renown that comparison and description are equally futile to do justice to the great Scene of Horsemanship and acrobatic power he daily enacts, it is styled

Newspaper advertisement for G. N. Eldred's Great Southern Circus and Menagerie, Montgomery Daily Advertiser, *December 13, 1859.*

for thirty-six hours before Queen Victoria saw them being fed. Whether Van Amburgh actually starved his valuable property is questionable, but there is no doubt that he followed the practice of the day to whip the lions violently to make them ferocious. Lion trainers routinely used loud noises to make the great cats roar and rage. To further excite audiences, lion trainers sometimes faked being mauled. The realization that the public would appreciate acts of skill, rather than ferocious acts, only came later in the century.[41]

In addition to circuses and menageries, Montgomerians attended smaller exhibits that had the air of the circus. Such performances must have existed from the earliest days, as a town ordinance of 1820 restricted "plays, games, tricks, juggling, sligh[sic] of hand, feats of dexterity or agility" on Sundays.[42] An 1835 ordinance established a license fee for "rope dancing, vaulting, tumbling, sligh [sic] of hand, juggling . . ."[43] Whereas spectacle and fear drew the masses to the circuses, physical and mental feats attracted the public to these smaller exhibits. The Cline Brothers, who did tightrope tricks of a high order, performed in Montgomery in January 1826. Monsieur Saubert, billing himself as "professor of experimental philosophy," presented a sort of magic show in December 1834. Chang and Eng, the Siamese twins, appeared at the Union Hotel for several days in mid-March 1834. In April 1843, Monsieur Paul, a French strong man, allowed a cannon to be fired while he was holding it. In the 1850s Herr Ryninger performed on a wire attached to the dome of the capitol. The former magician to Queen Isabel of Spain presented a "scientific" magic show in late January 1853. In March 1857 Signor Donetti's troupe of "learned" dogs, monkeys and goats attracted large, appreciative audiences in Montgomery. In No-

Newspaper advertisement for Nixon's Royal Circus, Montgomery Daily Advertiser, *November 13, 1860.*

vember, Chinese jugglers performed at Commercial Hall. In June 1859 an "aeronaut" and his balloon drifted eleven miles south of the city where men shot at the balloon. Beginning in 1855 with the opening of the thirty-acre fair grounds, jugglers, monkey shows and beauty contests, Indian curiosities and Siamese twins, fat ladies and skeleton men, and the hairy woman and two-headed girl appeared near agricultural produce and equipment, factory and home manufactures, and domestic and draft animals.[44]

Twenty-six year old Phineas T. Barnum's first traveling show was little more than such individual performances or exhibitions when he arrived in Montgomery in February 1837. His troupe was billed as Barnum's Grand Scientific and Musical Theatre, but it consisted only of a few performers. In addition to Barnum, who appeared as a black-faced singer and dancer, the troupe included a sleight of hand performer and a ventriloquist. Joe Pentland, who was later recognized as America's first great clown, played a comic. Considering the offering, it is understandable that Barnum did not do well financially. In December 1847 Barnum returned to Montgomery, this time on his way to Cuba. He had become a household name in America and Europe. On his recent European tour, Barnum had exhibited the midget General Tom Thumb, who had three command performances before Queen Victoria, as well as appearances for other crowned heads in Paris, Madrid and Brussels. In Montgomery Tom Thumb danced, sang, did imitations and even posed as Cupid and Hercules; he attracted very large crowds.

Barnum, the most successful promoter, knew that any publicity was better than none, that bigger was better, that the repeated slogan or method was effective, and that the public must always get its money's worth. But he did not manufacture public curiosity; he played to the public taste and subtly adapted his exhibits to the particular preferences of audiences. Like other promoters of circuses, menageries, and especially so-called freak shows, he aroused an already existing curiosity for the strange and bizarre. Animal and human curiosities, which were first exhibited individually, became an integral part of American circuses. Promoters may not have manufactured the interest in abnormalities, but they did play on the public's ignorance about what was normal. Consequently, little-known animals were exhibited as unfamiliar species, and even individuals from little-known lands were exhibited as anomalies, savages or some other species. And then of course, there were the true anomalies—and the faked ones.

Methods of presentation for individuals could change during their careers. Chang and Eng, the original "Siamese twins" were first presented as exotic; later in their careers, Western dress replaced Asian dress and pigtails. The public received Chang and Eng, like Tom Thumb, sympathetically, whereas the frightened and repulsed public often taunted the deformed and misshapen. Many believed that freaks' abnormalities were outward signs of

God's wrath and punishment for unknown sins.

Critics attacked circuses and menageries less often than the theater. Yet they met some antagonism when they began exhibiting in New York and New England in the 1820s—elephants were even shot and poisoned. To counter criticism, the Zoological Institute, an umbrella organization founded in 1835 by some one hundred twenty-five exhibitors, recommended advertising circuses and menageries as scientific and educational. Freak shows, presented in similar ways, were not criticized as distasteful, cruel or exploitative. The general public, and even the elite, accepted them. Scientists and physicians frequented the exhibits to examine the abnormalities, and in doing so, reinforced the pseudoscientific atmosphere the promoters were actively creating. What criticism there was came not because of any perceived impropriety, but because such amusements were frivolous.[45]

About 1840 the American Sunday School Union in Philadelphia issued a publication to teach the evils of life on the road.

> The men who belong to [the circus] are generally idle and worthless people, who move about from place to place, and get their living by taking money of many persons who cannot afford to spend it so foolishly. Then there is a great deal of drinking and gambling . . .[46]

The public viewed circus folk as rowdies, liars and cheats, because fights frequently occurred with locals and because many circus folk believed that anything was acceptable to make money. In the South, some public opinion mounted against the circuses because members of circus companies often freely mixed with slaves, thus raising the fear that the slaves might be incited to insurrection. Consequently, some circuses advertised themselves as being Southern companies, although none really were, and the Southern public viewed them all as being Northerners.

In 1860 *DeBow's Review* attacked circuses as fit only for children and blacks. Apparently elite opinion was turning against the most popular amusement of the time. The age of deference to church authority and social betters was past when menageries and circuses became widely popular in the United States. The elite may have regretted the diffusion of political, social, moral, aesthetic and religious authority, but the public liked circuses, and it patronized them. By the end of the antebellum period, the Jacksonian Age of the Common Man had passed, but the public had not given up the circus.[47]

Montgomery tried to control these events and to raise revenue from them by licensing fees. Impresarios complained and tried to have the fees waived; some succeeded, such as the People's Circus, which gave a benefit performance for the hospital fund, a cause selected by the city. City authorities charged proprietors to prevent or suppress disorderly conduct at their performances, and the police were allowed to attend free of charge. Well might the authorities have tried to intervene: Monsieur Adolphe Adrian, a juggler and sleight-of-hand artist, attempted to abduct the wife of Dr. J. R. McLeod. On May 12, 1840, the doctor caught, shot, and killed Monsieur Adrian at Huie's Ferry on the Alabama River.[48]

Minstrel Shows

From the 1840s onwards minstrel shows were the chief competition of dramatic performances. The preference of Montgomery's newspapers for the theater notwithstanding, the appeal of the minstrels seems to have been wide, for time after time they dominated the potential audience and threatened the theatrical companies' financial success.

Although precedents for black-face comedy existed, the country's first performance of a complete minstrel show dates from February 1843 when the Virginia Minstrels of New York presented an evening's entertainment of "oddities, peculiarities, eccentricities, and comicalities of that Sable Genus of Humanity."[49] Exaggerated or stereotypical caricatures of black mannerisms of moving, dancing, singing, speaking, and joking provided the humor of early minstrel shows.

These unpretentious shows had an air of spontaneity in that the minstrels could adapt the performance to the audience as the show progressed. This was possible because minstrel shows had no plots or musical scores; each element of the presentation stood alone. Audiences freely participated and expressed their delight or disapproval. Although the shows had no rigid structure, by the time they became popular in Montgomery most presentations had three parts and were less spontaneous than the earlier shows.

The shows opened with the minstrels seated in a semi-circle; they joked, sang and danced. The second part of the show, conducted in front of the curtain, consisted of acrobatics, singing, dancing and playing a variety of novelty musical instruments. The performance concluded with a one-act skit, usually set on a Southern plantation. Even with the inclusion of farces as afterpieces, theatrical performances could not match the rollicking good fun of the minstrel shows.

Minstrel shows targeted so-called aristocrats, physicians, professors and especially lawyers. The disapproval of minstrel shows evidenced in Montgomery newspapers could have been due to their anti-elitist tone. However, blacks provided the real focus of humor. Minstrels portrayed slaves as happy, loyal, carefree children, and free blacks in the North as lazy incompetents who, even if they did not want to return to slavery, should do so as they had no place in Northern society. Minstrel shows, a Northern invention, catered to the common man, especially to the recently-urbanized working classes of the large Northeastern cities, and served a psychological need for working men of the large cities. Audiences, however, were not restricted to one socioeconomic group; as early as 1844 minstrels performed at the White House, where they entertained presidents Tyler, Polk, Fillmore and Pierce. Although New York remained the center of minstrelsy throughout the antebellum period, minstrel shows were extremely popular all across the country, especially as the flexibility of the shows allowed them to be adapted to individual audiences.[50]

The Sable Melodists, a New Orleans and Mobile minstrel group, presented Montgomery's first recorded minstrel show. They delighted their patrons in mid-March 1849 and, with the Steyermarkesch Band, captured the majority of Montgomery's audience, leaving W. R. Hart's *Romeo and Juliet* poorly attended.

The Campbell Minstrels, the most popular minstrel show to appear in antebellum Montgomery, were routinely praised by Montgomery newspapers which generally preferred and promoted theatrical, musical and operatic performances, and relegated information about circuses and menageries, questionable exhibits and minstrel shows to paid advertisements. Montgomery's elite accepted the Campbell Minstrels, whereas they were not inclined to accept other minstrel companies. During the troupe's January 1855 run, a supper party in private rooms of the Exchange Hotel included the minstrels and Montgomerians, many of whom were ladies. Perhaps the company's ten-foot, three-inch African, previously an exhibit of Phineas T. Barnum, appealed to Montgomerians. Certainly, "The Plantation, Life Among the Happy," Campbell's pro-Southern version of *Uncle Tom's Cabin* that the troupe presented in New York during the spring and summer of 1854, appealed to Montgomery audiences. Minstrel companies capitalized on the popularity of anti-slavery and pro-Southern dramatic presentations of *Uncle Tom's Cabin*—both of which reinforced the almost universal belief in the United States that blacks were inferior beings who naturally should fill menial positions.

In January 1856 Campbell Minstrels' popularity and the internal weaknesses of William Crisp's theatrical company resulted in the minstrels' audience increasing as that of the theater decreased. In 1857 the Campbell Minstrels appeared in the winter, summer and fall. The unusual June run was probably because the Democratic State Convention was then meeting in Montgomery; the company included a thirteen-piece band for these summer performances. In the fall there were several attractions: horse races, the state agricultural fair, the theater, and the legislature. True to form Campbell's drew large audiences to the detriment of Duffield's theatrical company. In mid-May 1858 the Campbell Minstrels performed in Montgomery in conjunction with the Southern Commercial Convention and the Allen and Boothly Troupe, a theatrical group. The Campbell Minstrels returned in early December 1858 and again pleased Montgomerians. Each performance was preceded by a free brass band concert given in front of Concert Hall, the venue of the minstrel shows.

Campbell's was not the only minstrel troupe to appear in Montgomery. The public applauded the Boy Minstrels of Mobile during their three-day run in early June 1858.[51] Sanford's Opera Troupe of Philadelphia advertised a three-day stand in mid-December 1859. The advertisement billed Sam Sanford himself as the "greatest comedian of the age" and as the "pioneer of minstrelry" and the company as the "best troupe of minstrels in the world."[52] The promoters had not exaggerated. Minstrel companies did not travel to the extent that dramatic and operatic troupes did, because their great popularity allowed them to run for years in the large Northeastern cities. Sanford had performed for seven years in Philadelphia. In 1853 he wrote "Happy Uncle Tom," and sold scripts of "Sanford's Southern Version of *Uncle Tom's Cabin*" to other minstrel troupes. When Sanford appeared in Montgomery, he was including "Virginia Minstrels" in his performances, because audiences were interested in seeing the raucous exuberance that characterized minstrel shows of the mid-1840s. Less famous minstrels also played in Montgomery: New Orleans Minstrel Troupe in March 1860 and Ramsey and Newcomb's Minstrels that September.[53] The latter's advertisement touted a corps de ballet, pantomime troupe, "Ethiopian vocalists," the "best Negro Delineators and Comedians," and the "largest band ever concentrated together."[54] According to the *Advertiser's* editor, the Southern Minstrels, whose performances included songs, burlesques, "comicalities" and instrumental music "gave complete satisfaction."[55]

George Christy's Minstrels, who in 1847 became the most popular of all minstrel shows and ran for ten years in New York, played to large Montgomery audiences in November 1856 and again in January 1861. Christy combined the sentimental songs of Stephen F. Foster with the vitality of the early Virginia Minstrels. Although Christy was noted for his pro-Southern burlesque opera of *Uncle Tom's Cabin*, his position did not protect him when he tried to open in Charleston on December 20, 1860, South Carolina's "Independence Day." The troupe could only proceed with the show after the company's manager assured the audience that the performers were not sympathetic to the Union cause. The company slipped out of Charleston only to appear in Montgomery within two weeks.[56]

Minstrel shows were extremely popular across the country and in Montgomery, and most such shows, even those mounted in the North, were basically pro-Southern. Nevertheless, the editors of Montgomery newspapers, and probably the city's prominent citizens, could not wholeheartedly approve. Nationally, what support the elite had given minstrel shows declined in the late 1850s.[57] Minstrel shows were unabashedly anti-elite, and they certainly did not conform to standards of decorum or European standards of cultivation and sophistication aspired to by society. Furthermore, the elite

The original score of "Dixie" is held in the collections of the Alabama Department of Archives and History. Legend records that Daniel Emmett wrote the score on the wall of the Montgomery Theatre with a piece of charcoal and that Herman Arnold, Montgomery's German-born bandmaster, transcribed the minstrel music for band and played it at Jefferson Davis's inaugural parade in February 1861.

probably did not approve of the common man dictating standards of public entertainment. Yet, because of his numbers and because Montgomery could not support separate types of commercial entertainment, the common man did dictate what succeeded as entertainment in Montgomery.

Public entertainment began in Montgomery when there were nothing more than a few houses, stores and taverns standing in the forest beside the Alabama River. It began with several young professional men performing *Julius Caesar*. Their choice of Shakespeare, however, was not exclusively the choice of cultivated taste. Shakespeare appealed to the popular taste, especially in the modified versions of Shakespeare that predominated at the time. The distinction between cultured and popular taste was growing. As evidenced by newspaper articles, there was no distinct commercial entertainment for any one of Montgomery's socioeconomic groups—or for individual groups anywhere else except in a handful of Northeastern cities. Circuses and menageries made a pretense of being educational, but the public attended to be entertained. Minstrel shows made no pretense of being anything other than what they were—rough comic entertainment. The vast majority of theater and opera audiences supported these performances because they too provided for an evening's entertainment. A minority evaluated commercial entertainment on other grounds. Churches generally disapproved on moral bases. Some individuals, such as the newspaper editors, saw the theater, especially, as educational and morally uplifting, not merely entertaining. Although supporters and detractors of commercial entertainment were divided, the audiences were not. Spatial separation of popular and cultivated audiences and of popular and cultivated performances occurred only later in the century when sufficient numbers allowed for both audiences and tastes to be served separately. During the antebellum period Montgomerians, like their fellow Americans, shared a common commercial entertainment, yet the basis of appreciation of performances or types of entertainment was private, depending on individual taste and sophistication.

Conclusion

The loose collection of rude frame houses and cabins of 1819 became a city by 1861. County seat, state capital and provisional capital of the Confederacy, Montgomery was essentially a commercial center with manufacturing and industrial potential. Transportation and communications no longer depended on rafts and keel boats or the tortuous overland route by the Federal Road. The telegraph provided communications, regular steamboat service connected Montgomery and Mobile, and rail connections, already open to the east, were being extended to the south and west.

The city's wide major streets, still unpaved, were tree-lined and gaslighted. Seven houses of worship, including a Roman Catholic church and a Jewish synagogue, graced the city center—built of brick now after several disastrous fires. Wealthier citizens lived in Greek Revival and Italianate mansions set in spacious, landscaped grounds. Montgomery had no public park, but as in so many antebellum cities, the enclosed and landscaped cemetery provided a pleasant place to walk. Hotel reception rooms and a half dozen halls provided venues for balls, parties, lectures, exhibitions and musical performances; the luxurious new Montgomery Theatre seated about nine hundred. Several academies for boys and girls, a boarding school for young ladies, and a business school for young men, partially compensated for poor public schools.

As the population grew and diversified, socioeconomic differences, relatively insignificant during the fluid period of settlement, became more distinct. Socioeconomic mobility decreased, the elite entrenched, and a sizeable laboring-class white population emerged. Disparities of wealth grew more pronounced, and the middling classes began to coalesce into a distinct middle class.[1]

Antebellum Montgomerians, like other Americans, struggled to define appropriate uses of leisure time. Notwithstanding the general tendency to emphasize differences, antebellum Americans participated in similar leisure activities. The middling classes, with increased wealth and leisure time but few traditional leisure activities, had to define a leisure ethic, a task that was not completed before the first quarter of the twentieth century. Elites, however, had fewer dilemmas regarding appropriate leisure activities. Long-established upper classes, especially those of the South, were more inclined than any other segment of the population toward a free and unselfconscious use of leisure. However, the bulk of Montgomery's elite had only recently attained that status. Their values closely resembled those of new elites elsewhere, rather than older ones long accustomed to leisure. The new upper and middle classes were more likely to consider respectability and social ramifications in their choices of leisure activities than were the old elites—or the lower strata of society. Nevertheless, members of the old and new, Northern and Southern upper classes freely mixed, and their values, or at least behaviors, did not clash significantly. They summered together, especially at Saratoga in New York, and a few even intermarried.

Montgomerians, like other antebellum Americans, pursued a variety of leisure activities. Some turned to professional gambling and excessive drinking; others transformed hunting and fishing into sports. Hospitality—visiting, talking and eating together—dominated leisure time activities of all strata of antebellum American society. Grand hospitality, a practice of the elite, although associated with the South in fact and legend, was practiced by Northern elites as well. At the very end of the antebellum period, Montgomerians consciously altered New Year's open house to conform with the new, Northern social practice of "pop calling." Celebration of Thanksgiving and Christmas differed little; celebration of the Fourth of July followed what amounted to a national script, except at the end of the period when the military element was probably more evident in Montgomery than it was in the North. The state agricultural fair followed national trends, although the medieval tournament was a peculiar Southern event associated with the Cult of Chivalry—a value system that may have been more preached than practiced or understood, and that certainly was restricted to a relatively small group.

Commercial entertainment, which came to dominate American leisure time, became increasingly important during the antebellum period. Initially, the wealthy controlled thoroughbred horse racing, the first of the commercial entertainment. Trotting races made racing somewhat more egalitarian, but horse racing fell into national disfavor by the end of the period. Montgomerians saw the same plays, listened to the same music, attended the same circuses, and heard and saw similar—or slightly altered—minstrel acts. In many cases the human, animal and freak performers were the same ones who appeared in the North, or occasionally in Europe; national entrepreneurs had discerned what appealed to the broad American public. Nevertheless, religious and moral opposition to commercial entertainment continued throughout the period. Opposition in Montgomery, as elsewhere in the country, made commercial entertainment a risky undertaking, but the authorities were successful in proscribing commercial entertainment only in the early years in New England.

Fraternal organizations, volunteer military and fire companies, and a host of other voluntary associations—almost all with practical objectives—particularly appealed to urban men of the middling classes. Montgomery probably gave more attention to volunteer military companies than they received in the North, but perceived and real threats were closer at hand. Without doubt the proliferation of volunteer companies on the eve of secession was not paralleled in the North. The development of debating and literary societies, however, did parallel that experienced elsewhere, as societies founded for practical reasons and to support the work ethic gradually became forms of a somewhat sophisticated entertainment. The topics and issues that these societies addressed certainly reflected local interests; William Lloyd Garrison did not speak in Montgomery, but then abolition was certainly not universally popular in the North either. However, geographical reasons, not significantly differing values or tastes, can largely account for differences of who lectured or exhibited in Montgomery. In essence, the experiences antebellum Montgomerians had in defining appropriate leisure activities for the emerging middle class society conformed with experiences elsewhere. Antebellum white Montgomerians pursued the same leisure activities, with the notable exceptions of team sports and women's voluntary associations, that Northerners pursued.

Senator Wigfall's exaggerated statement to William Russell in May 1861 did not accurately describe Montgomery. By Eastern or European standards Montgomery remained very rough around the edges. After all, it was not long separated from its beginnings, a stage that all American cities experienced. Nevertheless, Montgomerians basically used their leisure time as their fellow urban Americans did. Availability, self-definition, and individual taste and aspirations determined what activities individuals selected. This aspect of Montgomery's antebellum culture did not differ significantly from that of urban centers elsewhere. In this regard, Senator Wigfall's statement was not strictly a statement of fact regarding the Confederacy or South as a whole, but a statement of propaganda, or at least an attempt to emphasize a distinct Southern cultural identity. War between conflicting cultures, rather than within a shared culture, was understandable and supportable, consequently what similarities there were had to be denied or ignored as irrelevant.

NOTES

INTRODUCTION

1 William Howard Russell, *My Diary North and South* (London: n.p., 1863; reprint ed., Philadelphia: Temple University Press, 1988), 130–31.

2 Patricia C. Clink, *The Spirit of the Times: Amusements in Nineteenth-Century Baltimore, Norfolk, and Richmond* (Charlottesville: University Press of Virginia, 1989), focuses on commercial entertainment from 1800 to 1870, "document[s] the evolution of nineteenth-century amusements and uncover[s] some of the reasons for the acceptance or rejection of certain amusements" [7] and finds that social class strongly influenced selection of particular leisure time activities. This book deals with similar evidence for antebellum Montgomery, but focuses on how Montgomerians used their leisure time and how their leisure time activities compared and contrasted with those of other urban Americans.

3 Matthew Powers Blue, *City Directory and History of Montgomery, Alabama, with a Summary of Events in that History, Calendarically Arranged, Besides Other Valuable and Useful Information* (Montgomery: T. C. Bingham & Co., 1878; second reprint ed., Montgomery: Society of Pioneers of Montgomery, 1971), 13–15, 34–36; Minnie Clare Boyd, *Alabama in the Fifties: A Social Study* (New York: Columbia University Press, 1931), 72–73, 79–81, 84–91; Clanton Ware Williams, "History of Montgomery, Alabama, 1817–1846" (Ph.D. dissertation, Vanderbilt University, 1938), 12–13, 169–74.

4 Blue, History, 8, 30; Leonard Mears and Turnbull, comp., *Montgomery City Directory, for 1859-'60* (Montgomery: Advertiser Book and Job Printing Office, 1859); Eighth Census of the United States, 1860: Agriculture, 2–5; *Eighth Census of the United States, 1860: Manufactures*, 9; Williams, "History of Montgomery, 1817–1846," 161–62; 174–77, Boyd, *Alabama in the Fifties*, 53–54; Harriet Martineau, *Society in America*, 2 vols. (London: Saunders & Otley, 1837; reprint ed., New York: AMS Press, 1966), I: 300–01.

5 The population of the city of Montgomery was:

YEAR	TOTAL	WHITES	BLACKS
1819	401	239	162
1830	1,450	800	650
1840	2,179	1,117	1,062
1850	8,728*	6,511*	2,217
1860	8,843	4,341	4,502

*The 1850 census seems to have been in error. Albert James Pickett, Alabama's first historian, wrote in 1852 that the city's population was then about six thousand, four thousand whites and two thousand blacks. Albert James Pickett, "A History of the City of Montgomery, Ala.," typescript of original manuscript deposited in the cornerstone of the Baptist Church, 10 March 1852, 7, A. J. Pickett Papers, Alabama State Department of Archives and History, Montgomery, Alabama.; Williams, "History of Montgomery, 1817–1846," 84, 145; *Sixth Census of the United States, 1840*; *Seventh Census of the United States, 1850*; George E. Waring, Jr., comp. *Report on the Social Statistics of Cities, Part II, The Southern and the Western States* (Washington: Government Printing Office, 1887; reprint ed., New York: Arno Press, 1970), 199; Thomas H. Clarke, "Montgomery," T. A. DeLand and A. Davis Smith, eds., *Northern Alabama: Historical and Bibliographical* (Chicago: Donohue and Henneberry, 1888), 589.

6 Williams," History of Montgomery, 1817–1846," 147; Warren Irvin Smith, "Structure of Landholdings and Slaveownership in Ante-Bellum Montgomery County, Alabama" (Ph.D. dissertation, University of Alabama, 1952), 44–50, 92–98, 106. Of the very few free blacks in Montgomery—seventy in 1860—only five were slave owners with three having a slave each and two owning two each.

7 Williams, "History of Montgomery, 1817–1846," 146–47; Smith, "Landholdings and Slaveownership in Ante-Bellum Montgomery County," 132–156; Emma Lila Fundaburk, "Business Corporations in Alabama in the Nineteenth Century," (Ph.D. dissertation, Ohio State University, 1963), 1224–78. Scholars have not adopted a standard terminology to describe "class" in antebellum America or even agreed if class accurately describes the socioeconomic stratification of most of antebellum America. See Stuart M. Blumin, "The Hypothesis of Middle-Class Formation in Nineteenth Century America: A Critique and Some Proposals," *American Historical Review* 90 (April 1985): 299–338, for an historiographical essay, and Stuart M. Blumin, *The Emergence of the Middle Class: Social Experience in the American City, 1760–1900* (Cambridge: Cambridge University Press, 1989), 230–35, 299–306; Bruce Collins, *White Society in the Antebellum South* (New York: Longman Group, 1985), 160–62; Robert H. Wiebe, *The Opening of American Society* (New York: Alfred A. Knopf, 1984), 322–24, 346–47; John S. Gilkeson, Jr., *Middle-Class Providence, 1820–1940* (Princeton: Princeton University Press, 1986), 3–4, 9; James Oakes, *The Ruling Race: A History of American Slaveholders* (New York: Alfred A. Knopf, 1982), 37–40. The use of the terms elite and middling classes in this book underscores the differences between the socioeconomic stratification in antebellum Montgomery and the much more rigid class divisions that were already significant in Northern cities at mid-century and were to dominate American society in the late nineteenth century.

8 *Eighth Census of the United States, 1860, Manuscript for Montgomery County, Alabama*, 1–93.

9 Blue, *History*, 51, 53, 88; Smith, "Landholding and Slaveownership in Ante-Bellum Montgomery County," 157, 160–62.

10 Anson West, *A History of Methodism in Alabama* (Nashville: Publishing House Methodist Episcopal Church, South, 1893; reprint ed., Spartanburg, S. C.: The Reprint Co., 1983), 347–53; Hugh Peter Young, "A Social and Economic History of Montgomery, Alabama, 1846–1860" (M.A. thesis, University of Alabama, 1948),

41; Pickett, "A History of the City of Montgomery, Ala.," 5; Blue, *History*, 16–17; Clarke, "Montgomery," 585; Hannah Simmon, ed., *The First 100 Years of Kahl Montgomery* (Montgomery: Paragon Press, 1952), 2–3; J. Wayne Flynt, "Alabama," in Samuel S. Hill, ed., *Religion in the Southern States: A Historical Study* (Macon: Mercer University Press, 1983), 5–6.

11 West, *Methodism in Alabama*, 348.

12 Eliza Goddard Whitman Pickett to Jane Whitman Bailey Keller, 27 November 1831, A. J. Pickett Papers, Alabama State Department of Archives and History, Montgomery, Alabama.

13 The Baptist Church first organized with six members in 1829, and reorganized with 17 in 1832—after the 1831 revival. The Methodist Episcopal Church had 49 white and 84 black members in 1838 and 134 white and 112 black members after the two 1839 revivals. The Presbyterians had 89 communicants in April 1845 and 118 the following April—after the 1845 revival. In April 1860 the Presbyterians had grown to only 186 communicants. Avery Hamilton Reid, *Baptists in Alabama: Their Organization and Witness* (Montgomery: Paragon Press for the Alabama Baptist State Convention, 1967), 50; Lee Norcross Allen, *The First 150 Years: Montgomery's First Baptist Church, 1829–1979* (Birmingham: Oxmoor Press for the First Baptist Church, 1979), 62–63; Marion Elias Lazenby, *History of Methodism in Alabama and West Florida* (n.p.: North Alabama Conference and Alabama-West Florida Conference of the Methodist Church, 1960), 250, 319; West, *Methodism in Alabama*, 585–86; James Williams Marshall, *The Presbyterian Church in Alabama* (Montgomery: Presbyterian Historical Society of Alabama, 129–33; Mattie Pegues Wood, *The Life of St. John's Parish: A History of St. John's Church from 1835–1955* (Montgomery: Paragon Press, 1955; reprint ed. with a 1990 supplement by J. Mills Thornton III. Montgomery: Black Belt Press, 1990), 3–9; Clanton Ware Williams, "Early Ante-Bellum Montgomery: A Black Belt Constituency," *Journal of Southern History 7* (November 1941): 503; Williams, "History of Montgomery, 1817–1846," 98–99, 104, 153–58; Young, "Social and Economic History, 1846–1860," 34–41; Boyd, *Alabama in the Fifties*, 159–3; Blue, *History*, 26, 82–84 87; Collins, *White Society in the Antebellum South*, 174; George Lewis, *Impressions of America and the American Churches: From Journal of the Rev. G. Lewis, One of the Deputation of the Free Church of Scotland to the United States* (Edinburgh: W. P. Kennedy, 1848; reprint ed., New York: Negro Universities Press, 1968), 158; Flynt, "Alabama," 9–10, 14; Wiebe, *The Opening of American Society*, 306–07; *Eighth Census of the United States, 1860, Statistics of the United States (Including Mortality, Property, Etc.)*, 352–54, listed 31 churches for Montgomery County with a seating capacity of 15,600; at the time the population of the county was 23,710 (12,122 whites; 11,802 slaves; 70 free blacks).

14 First Presbyterian Church, session book, 11 November 1843–18 July 1857, 11, 13, 17–18, 29–38, 65–67, 112; session book 1857–1869, 72; First Presbyterian Church Collection, Auburn University at Montgomery, Montgomery, Alabama; William James Mahoney, Jr., *One Hundred and Fifty Years: A Sesquicentennial History of the First Presbyterian Church* (Montgomery: Brown Printing Co, 1974), 8–9, 23; Walter C. Whitaker, *History of the Protestant Episcopal Church in Alabama, 1763–1891* (Birmingham: Roberts & Sons, 1898), 53, 66, 72–73, 124, 130; Solomon Franklin Smith, *Theatrical Management in the West and South for Thirty Years* (New York:

Harper & Bros., 1868), 108–09; Flynt, "Alabama," 9.
15 Diary of Mrs. Lucilla McCorkle, 1 May 1860, quoted in Collins, *White Society in the Antebellum South*, 179.
16 Whitaker, *Episcopal Church in Alabama*, 129.
17 La Margaret Turnipseed, "The Ante-Bellum Theatre in Montgomery, Alabama, 1840–1860" (M.A. thesis, Auburn University, 1948), 34–51; Boyd, *Alabama in the Fifties*, 187; Williams, "History of Montgomery, 1817–1846," 146, 160, 176.

Chapter 1

1 Foster Rhea Dulles, *America Learns to Play: A History of Popular Recreation, 1607–1940* (New York: D. Appleton-Century Co., 1940), 9–10, 13, 67–70, 85–91; Dale A. Somers, "The Leisure Revolution: Recreation in the American City, 1820–1920," *Journal of Popular Culture* 5 (Summer 1971): 125–128. In 1860 the overwhelming number of white Montgomerians lived in single family houses; a few lived in boarding houses. Additionally there were several traditional households that included workers employed by the head of household, for example Thomas Maker and his wife and two children, plus four stone masons, cutters and polishers; Wade Keys, lawyer, his wife and three children, plus eight law students; and G. Giovanni and his five hat makers. The most extreme example was that of Alfred A. Janney and his wife and four children, plus nineteen molders, carpenters, pattern makers and machinists who worked in his foundry. *Eighth Census of the United States, 1860, Manuscript for Montgomery County, Alabama*, 56, 67, 76, 80.
2 Albert James Pickett, "A History of the City of Montgomery, Ala.," typescript of original manuscript deposited in the cornerstone of the Baptist Church, 10 March 1852, 6, A. J. Pickett Papers, Alabama State Department of Archives and History, Montgomery, Alabama.
3 "Montgomery City Council Ordinances," January 1820, Alabama State Department of Archives and History, Montgomery, Alabama.
4 Ibid., 14 April 1829, 75; 22 February 1831, 92–93; March 1835, 134, 2 April 1849; *Montgomery Weekly Advertiser*, 18 July 1860; Robert H. Wiebe, *The Opening of American Society* (New York: Alfred A. Knopf, 1984), 330.
5 Patricia C. Clink, *The Spirit of the Times: Amusements in Nineteenth-Century Baltimore, Norfolk, and Richmond* (Charlottesville: University Press of Virginia, 1989), 57–71; Ann Fabian, *Card Sharps, Dream Books, and Bucket Shows: Gambling in 19th-Century America* (Ithaca: Cornell University Press, 1990), 1, 113–26; John M. Findlay, *People of Chance: Gambling in American Society from Jamestown to Las Vegas* (New York: Oxford University Press, 1986), 5–6, 44–78; Stephen Longstreet, *Win or Lose: A Social History of Gambling in America* (New York: Bobbs-Merrill Co., 1977), 37–40, 59–61.
6 *Acts of the General Assembly of the State of Alabama*, 1822, 76–77; 1834, 27–28; *Alabama Journal*, 17, 24 February 1826; "City Ordinances," 13 February 1843; Thomas H. Clarke, "Montgomery," T. A. DeLand and A. Davis Smith, eds., *Northern Alabama: Historical and Bibliographical* (Chicago: Donohue & Henneberry, 1888), 586–87; *Montgomery Advertiser and State Gazette*, 14 December 1854; Findlay, People of Chance, 40–43; Fabian, *Gambling in 19th-Century America*, 1, 113–26.

7 *Montgomery Republican*, 20 January 1821, as reported in Clarke, "Montgomery," 586; *Alabama Journal*, 21 October 1825; *Weekly Alabama Journal*, 12 February 1853; Fabian, *Gambling in 19th-Century America*, 3–4.

8 Fabian, *Gambling in 19th-Century America*, 13–14; *Acts of the General Assembly of the State of Alabama*, 1822, 26; 1826, 9; 1828, 73–74; 1834, 47; 1837, 24–25; 1854, 30.

9 Clarke, "Montgomery," 587–88; Solomon Franklin Smith, *Theatrical Management in the West and South for Thirty Years* (New York: Harper & Bros., 1868), 62; "Montgomery City Council Minutes," 28 February 1820, 23 January 1835, 19 May 1836, Alabama State Department of Archives and History, Montgomery, Alabama; "City Ordinances," [?] January 1820, [?] February 1828, 30 March 1830, 5 March 1831, 22 February 1831, 3 April 1834, February 1835, 25 February 1835, [?] March 1835, 5 February 1838, 29 February 1838, 30 November 1847, [?] July 1850; Findlay, *People of Chance*, 46–47, 63–70; Fabian, *Gambling in 19th-Century America*, 34–37; Thomas Cooper DeLeon, *Belles Beaux and Brains of the 60's* (New York: G. W. Dillingham Co., 1909), 54–55; Matthew Powers Blue, *City Directory and History of Montgomery, Alabama, with a Summary of Events in that History, Calendarically Arranged, Besides Other Valuable and Useful Information* (Montgomery: T. C. Bingham & Co., 1878; second reprint ed., Montgomery: Society of Pioneers of Montgomery, 1971), 28.

10 "City Ordinances," 25 February 1835.

11 *Montgomery Advertiser and State Gazette*, 14 December 1854.

12 Tyrone Power, Impressions of America During the Years 1833, 1834, and 1835, 2 vols. (London: R. Bentley, 1836), I: 100–01.

13 Walter Brownlow Posey, ed., Alabama in the 1830's As Recorded by British Travellers, Birmingham-Southern College Bulletin 31 (December 1938): 37, 41.

14 Roy Rosenzweig, *Eight Hours for What We Will: Workers and Leisure in an Industrial City, 1870–1920* (Cambridge: Cambridge University Press, 1983), 36; *Alabama Journal*, 20 June 1826; *Montgomery Daily Advertiser*, 9 September 1858, 5 January 1861; *Montgomery Weekly Post*, 31 October, 7, 14 November 1860; Daniel R. Hundley, *Social Relations in Our Southern States* (New York: Henry B. Price, 1860; reprint ed., Baton Rouge: Louisiana State University Press, 1979), 223–32; Dulles, *America Learns to Play*, 90.

15 "City Ordinances," [?] January 1820, 11 February 1829, 14 April 1829, 19 March 1834, 16 February 1835, [?] March 1835, 5 February 1838, 12 February 1838, [?] July 1850; *Montgomery Weekly Advertiser*, 28 March, 4 April 1860; *Montgomery Weekly Post*, 21 November 1860; James Benson Sellers, *The Prohibition Movement in Alabama, 1702 to 1943* (Chapel Hill: University of North Carolina Press, 1943), 29.

16 First Presbyterian Church, session book, 11 November 1843–18 July 1857, 13, 17–18, 29–38, 112, 131, First Presbyterian Church Collection, Auburn University at Montgomery, Montgomery, Alabama; Sellers, *Prohibition Movement in Alabama*, 14–39; Blue, *History*, 41, 43–44, 47–48, 52, 72, 87; Clanton Ware Williams, "History of Montgomery, Alabama, 1817–1846" (Ph.D. dissertation, Vanderbilt University, 1938), 152–53; Rosenzweig, *Eight Hours for What We Will*, 104; Clink, *The Spirit of the Times*, 77–81; Mark C. Carnes, *Secret Ritual and Manhood in Victorian America*

(New Haven: Yale University Press, 1989), 7; Wiebe, *The Opening of American Society*, 318; Mary P. Ryan, *Cradle of the Middle Class: The Family in Oneida County, New York, 1790–1865* (New York: Cambridge University Press, 1981), 134–35, 142; John S. Gilkeson, Jr., *Middle-Class Providence, 1820–1940* (Princeton: Princeton University Press, 1986), 35, 54.

17 Longstreet, *Win or Lose*, 59–61; David J. Pivar, *Purity Crusade: Sexual Morality and Social Control* (Westport, Conn.: Greenwood Press, 1973), 24–28, 32–34; Howard Brown Woolston, *Prostitution in the United States Prior to the Entrance of the United States into the World War* (Montclair, N.J.: Patterson Smith, 1969), 24–25; Fernando Heriques, *Prostitution and Society*, 2 vols. (New York: Citadel Press, 1965), II: 251–58, 270; Claudia D. Johnson, "That Guilty Third Tier: Prostitution in Nineteenth Century American Theaters," in Daniel Walker Howe, ed. *Victorian America* (Philadelphia: University of Pennsylvania Press, 1976), 118–20.

18 "City Ordinances," 19 February 1838, April 1842; *Montgomery Weekly Advertiser*, 24 October 1860, 5 January 1861; *Montgomery Weekly Post*, 5 December 1860.

19 *Montgomery Weekly Advertiser*, 5 September 1860. Certainly all brothels did not move out of the corporation limits. (In 1883 a new brothel was opened in violation of the 1875 city code proscribing prostitutes and bordellos; it was located just across the street from the Court Street Methodist Church, in the very heart of Montgomery, *Montgomery Daily Advertiser*, 19 July 1883.)

20 *Montgomery Weekly Advertiser*, 28 March 1860.

21 Ibid.

22 Ibid., 11 April 1860.

23 Ibid., 18 April 1860.

24 Donna R. Braden, *Leisure and Entertainment in America* (Dearborn, Mich.: Henry Ford Museum & Greenfield Village, 1988), 204; Dulles, *America Learns to Play*, 148; Hundley, *Social Relations in Our Southern States*, 31–41.

25 *Montgomery Daily Advertiser*, 25 May 1860; *Montgomery Weekly Post*, 3 October, 7, 14 November 1860; Leonard Mears and Turnbull, compilers, *Montgomery City Directory, for 1859-'60* (Montgomery: Advertiser Book and Job Printing Office, 1859), 80; Kathryn Grover, ed., *Hard at Play: Leisure in America, 1840–1940* (Amherst: University of Massachusetts Press, 1992), 79–80; Stephen Hardy, "'Adopted by All the Leading Clubs': Sporting Goods and the Shaping of Leisure, 1800–1900," in Richard Butsch, ed. For Fun and Profit: The Transformation of Leisure into Consumption (Philadelphia: Temple University Press, 1990), 75–76.

26 Hundley, *Social Relations in Our Southern States*, 34–40; Philip Henry Gosse, *Letters from Alabama, (U.S.) Chiefly Relating to Natural History* (London: Morgan & Chase, 1859), 50–51, 226–27, 266–70, 300–01.

27 Gosse, *Letters from Alabama*, 130.

28 Ibid., 131–32; Dulles, *American Learns to Play*, 70–71; *Weekly Alabama Journal*, 13 December 1856.

29 Minutes of the Bachelor's Club of the City of Montgomery, 21 June 1851–14 February 1860, 1–2, Alabama State Department of Archives and History, Montgomery, Alabama; *Weekly Alabama Journal*, 12 February, 5 March 1853; *Montgomery Weekly*

Advertiser, 9 May 1860; *Montgomery City Directory*, 105–08; Blue, *History*, 48. National societies also existed, such as the French Benevolent Society (founded 1830), Chevra Montgomery (founded 1846), and the St. Andrew's Society (founded 1860).

30 Blue, *History*, 47.

31 Ronald J. Zboray, *A Fictive People: Antebellum Economic Development and the American Reading Public* (New York: Oxford University Press, 1982), 105; Clarke, "Montgomery," 586; Ryan, *Cradle of the Middle Class*, 129–31.

32 Blue, History, 29; William Garrett, *Reminiscences of Public Men in Alabama for Thirty Years* (Atlanta: Plantation Publishing, 1872), 359–60, 595–97.

33 Zboray, *A Fictive People*, 107; Carl Bode, The *American Lyceum: Town Meeting of the Mind* (New York: Oxford University Press, 1956), 7–15.

34 Josiah Holbrook's October 1826 manifesto quoted in Bode, *American Lyceum*, 12.

35 Bode, *American Lyceum*, 7, 12, 27; Zboray, *A Fictive People*, 107–08.

36 Blue, *History*, 29, 53, 56, 58, 61; La Margaret Turnipseed, "The Ante-Bellum Theatre in Montgomery, Alabama, 1840–1860" (M.A. thesis, Auburn University, 1948), 24.

37 Bode, *American Lyceum*, 77, 83–85, 89, 110–19, 154, 160.

38 Ibid., 75–79, 119, 153–57, 160, 238, 240, 243, 250; Zboray, *A Fictive People*, 108.

39 Blue, *History*, 60, 44; *Eighth Census of the United States, 1860, Manuscript for Montgomery County, Alabama*; Clink, *The Spirit of the Times*, 29–30.

40 Boyd, *Alabama in the Fifties*, 220; *Montgomery Advertiser and State Gazette*, 2 January 1856; Hugh Peter Young, "Social and Economic History of Montgomery, Alabama, 1846–1860" (M.A. thesis, University of Alabama, 1948), 30; Turnipseed, "Ante-Bellum Theatre," 47.

41 Zboray, *A Fictive People*, 108; Blue, *History*, 49, 54–55, 57, 60; Clanton Ware Williams, "History of Montgomery, Alabama, 1817–1846" (Ph.D. dissertation, Vanderbilt University, 1938), 149–50; *Alabama Journal*, 29 March 1843; *Weekly Alabama Journal*, 10 April 1852.

42 *Montgomery Advertiser and State Gazette*, 20 January 1858, 13 April 1859; Blue, *History*, 43, 52–54, 57, 84, 87; Dulles, *America Learns to Play*, 93; Turnipseed, "Ante-Bellum Theatre," 18; Williams, "History of Montgomery, 1817–1846," 150; Robert O. Mellown, "Mental Health and Moral Architecture," *Alabama Heritage* 32 (Spring 1994): 10–11; Allen Johnson, ed., *Dictionary of American Biography*, 11 vols. (New York: Charles Scribner's Sons, 1964), X: 156–57, 643–44; Weibe, *The Opening of American Society*, 327–28.

43 Dulles, *America Learns to Play*, 92–95; Clink, *The Spirit of the Times*, 28–29; James H. Dormon, Jr., *Theater in the Ante Bellum South, 1815–1861* (Chapel Hill: University of North Carolina Press, 1967), 153.

44 George Francis Cushman, "The Characteristics & Aims of Freemasonry, An Address Deliver[e]d at the Public Installation of the Officers of Fulton Lodge, Fulton and Halo Lodge, Cahaba, Dallas County, Ala., On the Anniversary of St. John the Baptist, June 23rd, A. L. 5855," Selma, Ala.: Selma Reporter, 1855, Ralph Brown Draughon Library, Auburn University, Auburn, Alabama; *Alabama Journal*, 16, 30 December 1825, 9, 30 June, 7 July 1826; Ware, "History of Montgomery, 1817–1848," 107; Blue, *History*, 89.

45 *Alabama Journal*, 24 March, 7 July 1826, 1 July 1840; Montgomery Masonic Lodge No. 11 Returns, 1821–1828, 1842–1861; Montgomery Masonic Lodge No. 173 Returns, 1852–1861, Archives of the Grand Lodge of Free and Accepted Masons of Alabama, Montgomery, Alabama; William Preston Vaughn, *The Antimasonic Party in the United States, 1826–1843* (Lexington: University of Kentucky Press, 1983), 170–71; Joseph Abram Jackson, *Masonry in Alabama: A Sesquicentennial History, 1821–1971* (Montgomery: Brown Printing Co., 1970), 37–41, 43, 55–57, 60–61, 63, 169; Weibe, *The Opening of American Society*, 367–68; Ware, "History of Montgomery, 1817–1846," 107; *Montgomery City Directory*, 105; "Proceedings of the Annual Communication of the Grand Lodge of Alabama Held in the City of Montgomery, Commencing December 7th, 1857" (Montgomery: Barrett & Wimbish, 1858), Archives of the Grand Lodge of Free and Accepted Masons of Alabama, Millbrook, Alabama, 12–13.

46 Blue,*History* 48, 51; Jackson, *Masonry in Alabama*, 4, 8–11, 18–19; *Montgomery City Directory*, 105; Carnes, *Secret Ritual and Manhood in Victorian America*, 25–29.

47 Carnes, *Secret Ritual and Manhood in Victorian America*, 1–5, 11, 14, 24–29; Clink, *The Spirit of the Times*, 77; "Proceedings of the Grand Lodge of Alabama, 1857," 13–14.

48 Rollin G. Osterweis, *Romanticism and Nationalism in the Old South* (New Haven: Yale University Press, 1949), 55–56, 200; John H. Napier III, "Martial Montgomery: Ante-Bellum Military Activity," *Alabama Historical Quarterly* 29 (Fall and Winter 1967): 116.

49 Montgomery *Weekly Advertiser*, 4 April 1860.

50 Ibid.

51 Napier, "Martial Montgomery," 109–15, 121–27; Bruce Collins, *White Society in the Antebellum South* (New York: Longman Group, 1985), 143.

52 Napier, "Martial Montgomery," 111–15, 121–27; Blue, *History*, 19, 58; *Alabama Journal*, 11 May 1827; *Montgomery Weekly Advertiser*, 4 April 1860; *Montgomery Weekly Post*, 3, 31 October 1860.

53 Napier, "Martial Montgomery," 116–20; *Weekly Alabama Journal*, 12 July 1856; Montgomery Weekly Advertiser, 9 May 1860.

54 The Montgomery True Blues, Scrap book. Bart W. Lincoln, comp., 1910–1911, rebuilt 28 June 1939, January 1861 muster roll, Alabama State Department of Archives and History, Montgomery, Alabama; Napier, "Martial Montgomery," 127–28.

55 Williams, "History of Montgomery, 1817–1846," 66–67; Tennent L. McDaniel, *History of the Montgomery Fire Department, 1817–1926* (Montgomery: n. p., 1926), 4, 16.

56 *Montgomery Weekly Advertiser*, 31 October 1860.

57 McDaniel, *Montgomery Fire Department*, 11, 16–20, 28; Blue, *History*, 29, 62–63; *Montgomery Weekly Post*, 20 October 1860.

Chapter 2

1 Matthew Powers Blue, *City Directory and History of Montgomery, Alabama, with a Summary of Events in that History, Calendarically Arranged, Besides Other Valuable and*

Useful Information (Montgomery: T. C. Bingham & Co., 1878; second reprint ed., Montgomery: Society of Pioneers of Montgomery, 1971), 41–43, 81, 84–85, 87; *Montgomery Weekly Post*, 5, 19 December 1860.

2 Blue, History, 48, 82; *Montgomery Advertiser and State Gazette*, 14 December 1854, 18 November 1857, 13 December 1859, *Montgomery Weekly Advertiser*, 1 October, 7 November 1860; *Montgomery Weekly Post*, 17 October 1860; Theodore E. Stebbins, Jr., and Hermann W. Williams, Jr., *Encyclopedia of American Art*, Milton Rugoff, ed. (New York: E. P. Dutton, 1981), 12–13, 115–16, 128–29, 295.

3 "Montgomery City Council Minutes," 17 November 1856, Alabama State Department of Archives and History, Montgomery, Alabama; *Weekly Alabama Journal*, 24 November 1855, 29 November, 13 December 1856; Weymouth T. Jordan, *Ante-Bellum Alabama: Town and Country*, Florida State University Studies 27 (1957): 130–132; Patricia C. Clink, *The Spirit of the Times: Amusements in Nineteenth-Century Baltimore, Norfolk, and Richmond* (Charlottesville: University Press of Virginia, 1989), 30–31; *Harper's Weekly*, 27 November 1858.

4 Minnie Clare Boyd, *Alabama in the Fifties: A Social Study* (New York: Columbia University Press, 1931), 29; *Weekly Alabama Journal*, 24 November 1855, 14 November, 13 December 1856; *Montgomery Advertiser and State Gazette*, 18, 25 November 1857; *Harper's Weekly*, 27 November 1858; *Montgomery Advertiser*, 8 January 1911; Jordan, *Town and Country*, 132–36; Rollin G. Osterweis, *Romanticism and Nationalism in the Old South* (New Haven: Yale University Press, 1949), 3–4, 8, 13, 17, 55–56, 98–99, 215; Warren Irving Smith, "Structure of Landholdings and Slaveownership in Ante-Bellum Montgomery County, Alabama (Ph.D. dissertation, University of Alabama, 1952), 145.

5 *Alabama Journal*, 26 December 1828; *Montgomery Weekly Post*, 21, 28 November 1860; Donna R. Braden, *Leisure and Entertainment in America* (Dearborn, Mich.: Henry Ford Museum & Greenfield Village, 1988), 73.

6 *Montgomery Weekly Journal*, 26 December 1857.

7 *Alabama Journal*, 11 December 1839; *Weekly Alabama Journal*, 13 December 1856; *Spirit of the Times*, 18 January 1839, 8 January 1848, 26 January 1850.

8 *Daily Messenger*, 28 December 1857, quoted in Boyd, *Alabama in the Fifties*, 218.

9 Boyd, *Alabama in the Fifties*, 220–21.

10 *Montgomery Weekly Advertiser*, 5 January 1861.

11 *Montgomery Advertiser*, 8 January 1911; Braden, *Leisure and Entertainment*, 75.

12 *Weekly Alabama Journal*, 3 January 1857.

13 *Weekly Alabama Journal*, 18 October 1856, 13 December 1856; *Montgomery Weekly Post*, 5 December 1860; Blue, *History*, 43.

14 Hazel Butler Wible, "History of Montgomery, Alabama, 1860–1865" (M.A. thesis, Auburn University, 1939), 48; *Alabama Journal*, 6 November 1839; *Montgomery Advertiser*, 23 April 1841; Boyd, *Alabama in the Fifties*, 223; *Montgomery Daily Advertiser*, 9 September 1858.

15 Lee Norcross Allen, *The First 150 Years: Montgomery's First Baptist Church, 1829–1979* (Birmingham: Oxmoor Press for the First Baptist Church, 1979), 27; Anson West, *A History of Methodism in Alabama* (Nashville: Publishing House Methodist Episcopal

Church, South, 1893; reprint ed., Spartanburg, S. C.: The Reprint Co., 1983), 349–50; "Montgomery First Presbyterian Church Session Books," 11 November 1843–18 July 1857 and 1857–1869, 11, 13, 62, 65–71, 84, 112, 120, 123, 131, 145, 148, 151–52, First Presbyterian Church Collection, Auburn University at Montgomery, Montgomery, Alabama; Mattie Pegues Wood, *The Life of St John's Parish: A History of St. John's Church from 1834 to 1955* (Montgomery: Paragon Press, 1955; reprint ed. with a 1990 supplement by J. Mills Thornton III, Montgomery: Black Belt Press, 1990), 36; Walter C. Whitaker, *History of the Protestant Episcopal Church in Alabama, 1763–1891* (Birmingham: Roberta & Sons, 1898), 129.

16 Clanton Ware Williams, "History of Montgomery, Alabama, 1817–1846" (Ph.D. dissertation, Vanderbilt University, 1938), 106; Blue, *History*, 89; Leonard Mears and Turnbull, comp., *The Montgomery City Directory, for 1859-'60* (Montgomery: Advertiser Book and Job Printing Officer, 1859); *Alabama Journal*, 16 December 1825, 6 November 1839.

17 Frederick Law Olmsted, *A Journey in the Seaboard Slave States, with Remarks on Their Economy* (New York: Dix & Edwards, 1856), 554.

18 Ibid.

19 "City Council Minutes," 19, 22 December 1856; *Montgomery Weekly Post*, 12, 24 December 1860; *Montgomery Weekly Advertiser*, 7, 21 November, 5, 19, 26 December 1860, 5 January 1861.

20 Blue, *History*, 44; Thomas H. Clarke, "Montgomery," T. A. DeLand and A. Davis Smith, eds., *Northern Alabama: Historical and Bibliographical* (Chicago: Donohue & Henneberry, 1888), 579, 582, 586; *Alabama Journal*, 9 February 1827; *Weekly Alabama Journal*, 19, 26 February 1853; Foster Rhea Dulles, *America Learns to Play: A History of Popular Recreation, 1607–1940* (New York: D. Appleton Co., 1940), 162–63; John H. Napier, III, "Martial Montgomery: Ante-Bellum Military Activity," *Alabama Historical Quarterly* 29 (Fall and Winter 1967): 112, 117, 119–20.

21 Braden, *Leisure and Entertainment*, 43.

22 Blue, *History*, 66; "City Council Minutes," 10 June 1851; Clarke, "Montgomery," 581; *Alabama Journal*, 9 June, 7 July 1826, 10 July 1829.

23 Blue, *History*, 66.

24 "City Council Minutes," 10 June 1851; *Alabama Journal*, 10 July 1852; *Weekly Alabama Journal*, 17 July 1852.

25 *Montgomery Weekly Advertiser*, 11 July 1860.

26 Ibid.; *Montgomery Weekly Post*, 19 September 1860; *Eighth Census of the United States, 1860, Manuscript for Montgomery County, Alabama*, 5.

27 "Montgomery City Council Ordinances," January 1820-November 1835, [7] January 1820, 11 February 1829, 2 February 1835, Alabama State Department of Archives and History, Montgomery, Alabama.

28 *Alabama Journal*, 13 January 1821.

29 Ibid., 31 March 1826.

30 *Alabama Journal*, 14 October 1825, 12 May 1826, 26 December 1828.

31 John Hervey, *Racing in America, 1665–1825*, 2 vols. (New York: Scribners Press for

The Jockey Club, 1944), II: 91; Dale A. Somers, "The Leisure Revolution: Recreation in the American City, 1820–1920," Journal of Popular Culture 5 (Summer 1971): 134; John Rickards Betts, *America's Sporting Heritage: 1850–1950* (Reading, Mass.: Addison-Wesley, 1974), 12–13; John M. Findlay, *People of Chance: Gambling in American Society from Jamestown to Las Vegas* (New York: Oxford University Press, 1986), 38–39.

32 *Spirit of the Times*, 30 July 1836, 17 September 1836, 22 October 1836, 26 January 1850; Boyd, *Alabama in the Fifties*, 229–30.

33 *Alabama Journal*, 19 December 1828, 28 August 1832; *Spirit of the Times*, 17 February 1838, 18 January 1839, 19 November 1842.

34 *Spirit of the Times*, 9 February 1838.

35 Ibid., 17 February 1838.

36 *Alabama Journal*, 11 December 1839.

37 *Spirit of the Times*, 20 February 1841.

38 *Weekly Alabama Journal*, 10 July 1852; *Spirit of the Times*, 4 June 1853.

39 *Spirit of the Times*, 6, 13 June, 26 September 1857.

40 Ibid., 9 February 1838, 26 July 1851, 3 January 1852, 24 April, 22 May 1858, 17, 19 June, 20 November, 25 December 1858, 22 January, 12 February 1859, 21 January 1860; Dulles, *America Learns to Play*, 141; Clink, *The Spirit of the Times*, 69–70; Braden, *Leisure and Entertainment*, 200; Betts, *America's Sporting Heritage*, 12, 42–43.

41 Dulles, *America Learns to Play*, 139–41; Betts, *America's Sporting Heritage*, 17.

42 Allen, *Montgomery's First Baptist Church*, 27.

43 *Spirit of the Times*, 17 February 1838.

44 Ibid., 4 December 1858.

45 Montgomery Race Course Association, "Records," 1859–1860, 1, Alabama State Department of Archives and History, Montgomery, Alabama.

46 Ibid., 1–22.

47 *Montgomery Weekly Post*, 7 November 1860.

48 Clanton Ware Williams, "Early Ante-Bellum Montgomery: A Black Belt Constituency," *Journal of Southern History* 7 (November 1941): 504; Betts, *America's Sporting Heritage*, 16–17; *Spirit of the Times*, 26 September 1857, 8 October, 26 November 1859.

49 *Spirit of the Times*, 3 December 1859.

50 Ibid., 8 October 1859.

51 *Montgomery Advertiser*, 8 January 1911.

52 Hervey, *Racing in America*, 339; Betts, *America's Sporting Heritage*, 13–14.

53 Montgomery Race Course Association, "Records," 2–11, 15–16, 21. In 1866 the race course was sold to help pay debts of the association.

54 La Margaret Turnipseed, "The Ante-Bellum Theatre in Montgomery, Alabama, 1840–1860" (M.A. thesis, Auburn University, 1948), 14.

55 *Alabama Journal*, 5 August 1825, 22 June 1827, 17 April, 8 May 1839, 18 September, 13 November 1839, 30 July 1850; *Weekly Alabama Journal*, 17 July 1852, 5 July

1856; *Montgomery Advertiser and State Gazette*, 30 May 1855, 12 May, 17 June 1858; James F. Sulzby, Jr., *Historic Alabama Hotels and Resorts* (University: University of Alabama Press, 1960), 90–92, 209–10; George Edward Walton, *The Mineral Springs of the United States and Canada, with Analyses and Notes on the Prominent Spas of Europe, and a List of Sea-Side Resorts* (New York: D. Appleton & Co., 1873), 310.

56 Solomon Franklin Smith, *Theatrical Management in the West and South for Thirty Years* (New York: Harper & Bros., 1868), 116; Frank Lawrence Owsley, Jr., "Albert J. Pickett: Typical Pioneer State Historian" (Ph.D. dissertation, University of Alabama, 1955), 41; *Montgomery Advertiser and State Gazette*, 5 May 1858; Sulzby, *Historic Alabama Hotels and Resorts*, 229–32.

57 *Alabama Journal*, 1 July 1840; *Montgomery Advertiser and State Gazette*, 19 May, 16 June, 9 September 1858; Dulles, *America Learns to Play*, 149–53; Walton, *Mineral Springs of the United States*, 182; Sulzby, *Historic Alabama Hotels and Resorts*, 51–54, 90–92; Clink, *The Spirit of the Times*, 92–94; Kathryn, Grover, ed., *Hard at Play: Leisure in America, 1840–1940* (Amherst: University of Massachusetts Press, 1992), 78.

58 *Montgomery Advertiser and State Gazette*, 16, 17 June 1858; *Montgomery Weekly Advertiser*, 30 May 1860; Walton, *Mineral Springs of the United States*, 7, 221–22; Sulzby, *Historic Alabama Hotels and Resorts*, 125–26; Dulles, *America Learns to Play*, 149–50; Braden, *Leisure and Entertainment*, 291.

59 Billy Mac Jones, *Health-Seekers in the Southwest, 1817–1900* (Norman: University of Oklahoma Press, 1967), 18–19; Clink, *The Spirit of the Times*, 88–99; Dulles, *America Learns to Play*, 149–50, 156; Stuart M. Blumin, *The Emergence of the Middle Class: Social Experience in the American City, 1760–1900* (Cambridge: Cambridge University Press, 1989), 231, 299–308.

CHAPTER 3

1 Patricia C. Clink, *The Spirit of the Times: Amusements in Nineteenth-Century Baltimore, Norfolk, and Richmond* (Charlottesville: University Press of Virginia, 1989), 1–5; James H. Dormon, Jr., *Theater in the Ante Bellum South, 1815–1861* (Chapel Hill: University of North Carolina Press, 1967), x, 231–37, 250–1, 256–59, 280; Lawrence W. Levine, *Highbrow/Lowbrow: The Emergence of Cultural Hierarchy in America* (Cambridge: Harvard University Press, 1988), 9, 86, 96–99; Foster Rhea Dulles, *America Learns to Play: A History of Popular Recreation, 1607–1940* (New York: D. Appleton Co., 1940), 100–03; Charles S. Watson, *The History of Southern Drama* (Lexington: University Press of Kentucky, 1997), 10–74.

2 Matthew Powers Blue, *City Directory and History of Montgomery, Alabma, with a Summary of Events in that History, Calendarically Arranged, Besides Other Valuable and Useful Information* (Montgomery: T. C. Bingham & Co., 1878; second reprint ed., Montgomery: Society of Pioneers of Montgomery, 1971), 12–13, 61, 88; Henry Welch Adams, *The Montgomery Theatre, 1822–1835*, University of Alabama Studies 9 (September 1955), 2–3, 10–12, 43; William Garrett, *Reminiscences of Public Men in Alabama for Thirty Years* (Atlanta: Plantation Publishing, 1872), 614–15; "Montgomery City Council Minutes," licenses for 1820, Alabama State Department of Archives and History, Montgomery, Alabama; "Montgomery City Ordinances," 14, 28 January 1820, Alabama State Department of Archives and History, Montgomery,

Alabama; *Montgomery Republican*, 28 May 1823.

3 Noah Miller Ludlow, *Dramatic Life As I Knew It* (St. Louis, 1880; reprint ed., New York: Benjamin Blom, 1966), 303.

4 Adams, *Montgomery Theatre*, 11–18, 28–29, 37, 43–44; Dormon, *Theater in the Ante Bellum South*, 117; Ludlow, *Dramatic Life*, 336; Solomon Franklin Smith, *Theatrical Management in the West and South for Thirty Years* (New York: Harper & Bro., 1868), 62–63, 77, 110; Blue, *History*, 45; Benjamin Buford Williams, *A Literary History of Alabama: The Nineteenth Century* (Cranbury, N. J.: Associated University Presses, 1979), 139; Watson, *Southern Drama*, 49–51.

5 Smith, *Theatrical Management*, 109.

6 Clink, *The Spirit of the Times*, 40; Dormon, *Theater in the Ante Bellum South*, 231–51; Dulles, *America Learns to Play*, 104–05; John F. Kasson, *Rudeness and Civility: Manners in Nineteenth-Century Urban America* (New York: Hill & Wang, 1990), 215–21; Bruce A. McConachie, "Pacifying American Theatrical Audiences, 1820–1900," in Richard Butsch, ed., *For Fun and Profit: The Transformation of Leisure into Consumption* (Philadelphia: Temple University Press, 1990), 49.

7 Smith, *Theatrical Management*, 62, 108–09, 208–09.

8 *Alabama Journal*, 28 October 1825.

9 Ibid., 4 November 1825.

10 Dulles, *America Learns to Play*, 89; Thomas M. Owen, "The Methodist Churches of Montgomery" (Montgomery: Paragon Press, 1908), 8–9; Blue, *History*, 21; Dormon, *Theater in the Ante Bellum South*, 116; Eliza Goddard Whitman Pickett to Jane Whitman Bailey Keller, 27 November 1831, A. J. Pickett Papers, Alabama State Department of Archives and History, Montgomery, Alabama.

11 Smith, *Theatrical Management*, 109.

12 Ibid.

13 Lee Norcross Allen, *The First 150 Years: Montgomery's First Baptist Church, 1829–1979* (Birmingham: Oxmoor Press for the First Baptist Church, 1979), 27.

14 Ibid., 28–29.

15 *Montgomery Weekly Advertiser*, 14 November 1860.

16 Katherine K. Preston, *Opera on the Road: Traveling Opera Troupes in the United States, 1825–1860* (Chicago: University of Illinois Press, 1993), 116–17; Dormon, *Theater in the Ante Bellum South*, 151–53; *Alabama Journal*, 24 April 1839; La Margaret Turnipseed, "The Ante-Bellum Theatre in Montgomery, Alabama, 1840–1860" (M.A. thesis, Auburn University, 1948), 10–15; Owen, "Methodist Churches," 10; Allen, *Montgomery Theatre*, 28, 39–40; Blue, *History*, 26.

17 Turnipseed, "Ante-Bellum Theatre," 16–22, 25–32; Mattie Pegues Wood, *The Life of St. John's Parish: A History of St. John's Church from 1834 to 1955* (Montgomery: Paragon Press, 1955; reprint ed. with a 1990 supplement by J. Mills Thornton III. Montgomery: Black Belt Press, 1990), 3–9, 13–14; Clanton Ware Williams, "History of Montgomery, Alabama, 1817–1846" (Ph.D. dissertation, Vanderbilt University, 1938), 153–57; Hugh Peter Young, "A Social and Economic History of Montgomery, Alabama, 1846–1860" (M.A. thesis, University of Alabama, 1948), 37; Avery Hamilton Reid, *Baptists in Alabama: Their Organization and Witness* (Montgomery: Paragon

Press for the Baptist State Convention, 1967), 50; Blue, *History*, 53.
18 Turnipseed, "Ante-Bellum Theatre," 32–51; Dormon, *Theater in the Ante Bellum South*, 168–72; *Weekly Alabama Journal*, 12 February 1853; Carl Bode, *The Anatomy of American Popular Culture, 1840–1861* (Berkeley: University of California Press, 1960), 4.
19 *Weekly Alabama Journal*, 22 January 1853.
20 Turnipseed, "AnteBellum Theatre," 47, 53–62, 65–73.
21 *Montgomery Weekly Post*, 17 October 1860.
22 Dormon, *Theater in the Ante Bellum South*, Dulles, *America Learns to Play*, 106–07; Clink, *The Spirit of the Times*, 35–38, 41–45; Levine, *Highbrow/Lowbrow*, 9; Claudia D. Johnson, "That Guilty Third Tier: Prostitution in Nineteenth Century American Theaters," Daniel Walker Howe, ed., *Victorian America* (Philadelphia: University of Pennsylvania Press, 1976), 111–20.
23 *Montgomery Weekly Advertiser*, 12 September 1860; biographical information here and elsewhere in this chapter is supplemented by Allen Johnson, ed., *Dictionary of American Biography* (New York: Charles Scribner's Sons, 1964).
24 *Montgomery Weekly Post*, 24 October 1860.
25 *Montgomery Weekly Advertiser*, 28 November, 5, 19, 26 December 1860; Bode, *American Popular Culture*, 7; Dormon, *Theater in the Ante Bellum South*, 248–49, 257–58; Clink, *The Spirit of the Times*, 48–49; *Montgomery Weekly Post*, 31 October, 14, 19 November 1860.
26 Watson, *Southern Drama*, 64–67; Clink, *The Spirit of the Times*, 35, 46–48, 50; Dormon, *Theater in the Ante Bellum South*, 252–80; Dulles, *America Learns to Play*, 100–03, 111; Bode, *American Popular Culture*, 6–7; Kasson, Rudeness and Civility, 215–18; Levine, *Highbrow/Lowbrow*, 3–4, 13–16, 34–37; Adams, *Montgomery Theatre*, 38–42; Preston, *Opera on the Road*, 1–2; Maud and Otis Skinner, *One Man in His Time: The Adventures of H. Watkins, Strolling Player, 1845–1863, From His Journal* (Philadelphia: University of Pennsylvania Press, 1938), 117–18.
27 Turnipseed, "Ante-Bellum Theatre," 43, 48, 68; Blue, *History*, 48, 54, 83; Clanton Williams, "History of Montgomery, 1817–1846," 150; *Weekly Alabama Journal*, 19 March 1853; *Montgomery Advertiser and State Gazette*, 6 Februrary 1856; Minnie Clare Boyd, *Alabama in the Fifties: A Social Study* (New York: Columbia University Press, 1931), 226; Neil Harris, *Humbug: The Art of P. T. Barnum* (Boston: Little, Brown & Co., 1973), 120–41; Preston, *Opera on the Road*, 29, 390.
28 Smith, *Theatrical Management*, 63.
29 Ibid., 62–63; Preston, *Opera on the Road*, 5, 25–26, 75, 106–07, 230–34, 383; Blue, *History*, 54; Turnipseed, "Ante-Bellum Theatre," 48.
30 Turnipseed, "Ante-Bellum Theatre," 29–30, 63–65; Preston, *Opera on the Road*, 142, 145–47, 244, 247–48, 306–16, 348, 366, 396; Boyd, *Alabama in the Fifties*, 31–32, 226; June C. Ottenberg, *Opera Odyssey: Towards a History of Opera in Nineteenth-Century America* (Westport, Conn.: Greenwood Press, 1994), 62–63, 107; Young, "Social and Economic History, 1846–1860," 25–26; *Weekly Alabama Journal*, 19 February 1853, 22 November 1856; Harris, *Humbug*, 97, 113; Blue, *History*, 57; Bode, *American Popular Culture*, 31–32.

31 Turnipseed, "Ante-Bellum Theatre," 65, 68; Preston, *Opera on the Road*, 100, 138–41, 213, 256–59, 350; Hazel Butler Wible, "History of Montgomery, Alabama, 1860–1865" (M.A. thesis, Auburn University, 1939), 121–22; Ottenburg, *Opera Odyssey*, 77–78, 89–90; Clink, *The Spirit of the Times*, 42–43; Frederick Law Olmsted, *A Journey in the Seaboard Slave States, with Remarks on Their Economy* (New York: Dix & Edwards, 1856), 552; Levine, *Highbrow/Lowbrow*, 63–69.

32 *Alabama Journal*, 9 January 1829; Blue, *History*, 42, 50; Clanton Williams, "History of Montgomery, 1817–1846," 151; Marian Murray, *Circus! From Rome to Ringling* (Westport, N. Y.: Greenwood Press, 1956), 130–31, 134; Clink, *The Spirit of the Times*, 23–27.

33 *Alabama Journal*, 23 December 1840; Blue, *History*, 8.

34 Robert Bogham, *Freak Show: Presenting Human Oddities for Amusement and Profit* (Chicago: University of Chicago Press, 1988), 26–27; Harris, *Humbug*, 23.

35 *Weekly Alabama Journal*, 21 December 1850; M. J. Gladstone, "Circus Wagons," in Milton Rugoff, ed., *Encyclopedia of American Art*, (New York: E. P. Dutton, 1981), 117–18.

36 *Weekly Alabama Journal*, 21 December 1850.

37 *Alabama Journal*, 18 April 1851.

38 Turnispeed, "Ante-Bellum Theatre," 50; Murray, *Circus!*, 166–70; Dormon, *Theater in the Ante Bellum South*, 113; Gladstone, "Circus Wagons," 118.

39 *Montgomery Advertiser and State Gazette*, 13 February 1856.

40 *Montgomery Mail*, 7 March 1859; Blue, *History*, 45.

41 Murray, *Circus!*, 135–38, 191–92, 260.

42 "Montgomery City Council Ordinances," [?] January 1820.

43 Ibid., 29 June 1835.

44 Clink, *The Spirit of the Times*, 24–25; Adams, *Montgomery Theatre*, 17, 34–35, 63–64; Blue, *History*, 2, 51–52, 56, 58, 84; Williams, "History of Montgomery," 150–51; Turnispeed, "Ante-Bellum Theatre," 31; Boyd, *Alabama in the Fifties*, 229; *Weekly Alabama Journal*, 22 January 1853; *Mobile Daily Register*, 5 March 1853; Young, "Social and Economic History, 1846–1860," 22–23; Weymouth T. Jordan, *Ante-Bellum Alabama: Town and Country*, Florida State University Studies 27, 1957, 130–33.

45 Murray, *Circus!*, 131–32, 143–44, 147, 155–57; Phineas Taylor Barnum, *Struggles and Triumphs: or, Forty Years' Recollections of P. T. Barnum* (New York: American News Co., 1871), 100–01, 173, 259; Harris, *Humbug*, 27, 49, 89, 93–101, 108; Blue, *History*, 85–86; Bogham, *Freak Show*, 25–27, 41, 62, 115.

46 American Sunday School Union, c. 1840, quoted in Bogham, *Freak Show*, 78.

47 Bogham, *Freak Show*, 78–93; Turnispeed, "Ante-Bellum Theatre," 45, 49; Harris, *Humbug*, 3, 74–75, 93; Murray, *Circus!*, 170.

48 "Montgomery City Council Ordinances," 4 January 1827, 29 June 1835, 29 January 1938, 16 April 1849; "Montgomery City Council Minutes," 1 April 1851; Young, "Social and Economic History, 1846–1860," 21–22; Blue, *History*, 60.

49 Virginia Minstrels 1844 program quoted in Robert C. Toll, *Blacking Up: The Minstrel Show in Nineteenth-Century America* (New York: Oxford University Press, 1974), 30.

50 Toll, *Minstrel Show*, 31, 33–36, 43–48, 52–57, 65–73.
51 Blue, *History*, 45, 53, 81; Turnipseed, "Ante-Bellum Theatre," 28–29, 42–43, 46–47, 55–56, 59, 61–63; Toll, *Minstrel Show*, 136, 90–95; Turnipseed, "Ante-Bellum Theatre," 46–47, 55–56, 59, 61–63; *Montgomery Advertiser and State Gazette*, 30 January 1856.
52 *Montgomery Daily Advertiser*, 13 December 1859.
53 Toll, *Minstrel Show*, 32, 94–95, 155; *Montgomery Weekly Advertiser*, 28 March 1860.
54 *Montgomery Weekly Post*, 26 September 1860.
55 *Montgomery Weekly Advertiser*, 26 December 1860.
56 Blue, *History*, 81; *Montgomery Weekly Post*, 19 December 1860; *Montgomery Weekly Advertiser*, 5 January 1861; Toll, *Minstrel Show*, 32, 37–38, 93–94, 104–05; Watson, *Southern Drama*, 65.
57 Clink, *The Spirit of the Times*, 53.

Conclusion

1 Montgomery has no scholarly history. The best two sources for information on Montgomery at the end of the antebellum period are Hugh Peter Young's, "A Social and Economic History of Montgomery, Alabama, 1846–1860" (M.A. thesis, University of Alabama, 1948), and Mary Ann Neeley's annotated version of Matthew Powers Blue, *The Works of Matthew Blue, Montgomery's First Historian* (Montgomery: NewSouth Books, 2010).

Bibliography

Except as noted, all documents are in the Alabama State Department of Archives and History, Montgomery, Alabama.

Primary Sources

Special Collections

Bachelor's Club of the City of Montgomery, minutes, 21 June 1851–14 February 1860.
Cushman, George Francis. "The Characteristics & Aims of Freemasonry, An Address Deliver[e]d at the Public Installation of the Officers of Fulton Lodge, Fulton and Halo Lodge, Cahaba, Dallas County, Ala., On the Anniversary of St. John the Baptist, June 23rd, A. L., 5855." Selma, Ala.: *The Selma Reporter*, 1855. Ralph Brown Draughon Library, Auburn University, Auburn, Alabama.
First Presbyterian Church, session books, 11 November 1843–18 July 1857 and 1857–1869. First Presbyterian Church Collection, Auburn University at Montgomery, Montgomery, Alabama.
McJunkin, James Bell. "The Church Record; or Session Book of the Presbyterian Church; at Montgomery, Alabama," November 1840. First Presbyterian Church Collection, Auburn University at Montgomery, Montgomery, Alabama.
Montgomery Masonic Lodge No. 11 Returns, 1821–1828, 1842–1861, Archives of the Grand Lodge of Free and Accepted Masons of Alabama, Millbrook, Alabama.
Montgomery Masonic Lodge No. 173 Returns, 1852–1861, Archives of the Grand Lodge of Free and Accepted Masons of Alabama, Millbrook, Alabama.
Montgomery Race Course Association, records, 1859–1860.
The Montgomery True Blues, Scrap book. Bart W. Lincoln, comp., 1910–1911, rebuilt 28 June 1939.
Pickett, Albert James. "A History of the City of Montgomery, Ala." 1852. Typescript of original manuscript deposited in the cornerstone of the Baptist Church, 10 March 1852. A. J. Pickett Papers.
Pickett, Eliza Goddard Whitman to Jane Whitman Bailey Keller, 27 November 1831, A. J. Pickett Papers.
"Proceedings of the Annual Communication of the Grand Lodge of Alabama Held

in the City of Montgomery, Commencing December 7th, 1857." Montgomery: Barrett & Wimbish, 1858. Archives of the Grand Lodge of Free and Accepted Masons of Alabama, Millbrook, Alabama.

Contemporary Periodicals

Unless otherwise noted, all documents are in the Alabama State Department of Archives and History, Montgomery, Alabama.
Alabama Journal, 13 January 1826–10 July 1852 (scattered)
Harper's Weekly, 27 November 1858.
Mobile Daily Register, 5 March 1853.
Montgomery Advertiser, 23 April 1841, 2 July 1882, 19 July 1883, 8 January 1911.
Montgomery Advertiser and State Gazette, 14 December 1854–13 April 1859.
Montgomery Daily Advertiser, 9 September 1858–5 January 1861.
Montgomery Mail, 7 March 1859.
Montgomery Weekly Advertiser, 28 March 1860–5 January 1861.
Montgomery Weekly Post, 30 March 1860–24 December 1860.
Spirit of the Times, New York City weekly, 5 June 1836–17 November 1860. Ralph Brown Draughon Library, Auburn University, Auburn, Alabama.
Weekly Alabama Journal, 21 December 1850–3 January 1857.

Public Records and Documents

Acts Passed at the Annual Session of the General Assembly of the State of Alabama, 1822, 1826, 1828, 1834, 1837, 1854.
Eighth Census of the United States, 1860.
Fifth Census of the United States, 1830.
Fourth Census of the United States, 1820.
Seventh Census of the United States, 1850.
Sixth Census of the United States, 1840.
Montgomery, Ala. "Montgomery City Council," minutes, 1820–1860. Alabama State Department of Archives and History, Montgomery, Alabama.
Montgomery, Ala. "Montgomery City Council," ordinances, January 1820-November 1835; January 1838-July 1850. Alabama State Department of Archives and History, Montgomery, Alabama.
The Montgomery City Directory, for 1859-'60. Compiled by Leonard Mears and Turnbull. Montgomery: Advertiser Book and Job Printing Office, 1859. Alabama State Department of Archives and History, Montgomery, Alabama.
Waring, George E., Jr., comp. *Report on the Social Statistics of Cities, Part II, The Southern and the Western States*. Washington: Government Printing Office, 1887; reprint ed., New York: Arno Press, 1970.

Diaries, Histories, Reminiscences, Memoirs

Barnum, Phineas Taylor. *Struggles and Triumphs: or, Forty Years' Recollections of P. T. Barnum.* New York: American News Co., 1871.

Blue, Matthew Powers. *City Directory and History of Montgomery, Alabama, with a Summary of Events in that History, Calendarically Arranged, Besides Other Valuable and Useful Information.* Montgomery: T. C. Bingham & Co., 1878; second reprint ed., Montgomery: Society of Pioneers of Montgomery, 1971.

Garrett, William. *Reminiscences of Public Men in Alabama for Thirty Years.* Atlanta: Plantation Publishing, 1872.

Gosse, Philip Henry. *Letters from Alabama, (U.S.) Chiefly Relating to Natural History.* London: Morgan & Chase, 1859.

Hundley, Daniel R. *Social Relations in Our Southern States.* New York: Henry B. Price, 1860; reprint ed., Baton Rouge: Louisiana States University Press, 1979.

Lewis, George. *Impressions of America and the American Churches: From Journal of the Rev. G. Lewis, One of the Deputation of the Free Church of Scotland to the United States.* Edinburgh: W. P. Kennedy, 1848; reprint ed., New York: Negro Universities Press, 1968.

Ludlow, Noah Miller. *Dramatic Life As I Found It.* St. Louis, 1880; reprint ed., New York: Benjamin Blom, 1966.

Martineau, Harriet. *Society in America.* 2 vols. London: Saunders & Otley, 1837; reprint ed., New York: AMS Press, 1966.

Olmsted, Frederick Law. *A Journey in the Seaboard Slave States, with Remarks on Their Economy.* New York: Dix & Edwards, 1856.

Power, Tyrone. *Impressions of America During the Years 1833, 1834, and 1835.* 2 vols. London: R. Bentley, 1836.

Russell, William Howard. *My Diary North and South.* London: n. p., 1863; reprint ed., Philadelphia: Temple University Press, 1988.

Smith, Soloman Franklin. *Theatrical Management in the West and South for Thirty Years.* New York: Harper & Bros., 1868.

SECONDARY SOURCES

Books

Adams, Henry Welch. *The Montgomery Theatre, 1822–1835.* University of Alabama Studies 9, September 1955.

Allen, Lee Norcross. *The First 150 Years: Montgomery's First Baptist Church, 1829–1979.* Birmingham: Oxmoor Press for the First Baptist Church, 1979.

Betts, John Rickards. *America's Sporting Heritage: 1850–1950.* Reading, Mass.: Addison-Wesley Publishing Co., 1974.

Blumin, Stuart M. *The Emergence of the Middle Class: Social Experience in the American City, 1760–1900.* Cambridge: Cambridge University Press, 1989.

Bode, Carl. *The American Lyceum: Town Meeting of the Mind*. New York: Oxford University Press, 1956.

Bogham, Robert. *Freak Show: Presenting Human Oddities for Amusement and Profit*. Chicago: University of Chicago Press, 1988.

Boyd, Minnie Clare. *Alabama in the Fifties: A Social Study*. New York: Columbia University Press, 1931.

Braden, Donna R. *Leisure and Entertainment in America*. Dearborn, Mich.: Henry Ford Museum & Greenfield Village, 1988.

Carnes, Mark C. *Secret Ritual and Manhood in Victorian America*. New Haven: Yale University Press, 1989.

Clink, Patricia C. *The Spirit of the Times: Amusements in Nineteenth-Century Baltimore, Norfolk, and Richmond*. Charlottesville: University Press of Virginia, 1989.

Collins, Bruce. *White Society in the Antebellum South*. New York: Longman Group, 1985.

DeLeon, Thomas Cooper. *Belles Beaux and Brains of the 60's*. New York: G. W. Dillingham Co., 1909.

Dormon, James H., Jr. *Theater in the Ante Bellum South, 1815–1861*. Chapel Hill: University of North Carolina Press, 1967.

Dulles, Foster Rhea. *America Learns to Play: A History of Popular Recreation, 1607–1940*. New York: D. Appleton-Century Co., 1940.

Fabian, Ann. *Card Sharps, Dream Books, and Bucket Shops: Gambling in 19th-Century America*. Ithaca: Cornell University Press, 1990.

Findlay, John M. *People of Chance: Gambling in American Society from Jamestown to Las Vegas*. New York: Oxford University Press, 1986.

Gilkeson, John S., Jr. *Middle-Class Providence, 1820–1940*. Princeton: Princeton University Press, 1986.

Griffith, Lucille, ed *History of Alabama, 1540–1900, As Recorded In Diaries, Letters, and Papers of the Times*. Northport, Ala.: Colonial Press, 1962.

Grover, Kathryn, ed. *Hard at Play: Leisure in America, 1840–1940*. Amherst: University of Massachusetts Press, 1992.

Harris, Neil. *Humbug; The Art of P. T. Barnum*. Boston: Little, Brown & Co., 1973.

Henriques, Fernando. *Prostitution and Society*. 2 vols. New York: Citadel Press, 1965.

Hervey, John. *Racing in America, 1665–1865*. 2 vols. New York: Scribners Press for The Jockey Club, 1944.

Jackson, Joseph Abram. *Masonry in Alabama: A Sesquicentennial History, 1821–1971*. Montgomery: Brown Printing Co., 1970.

Johnson, Allen, ed. *Dictionary of American Biography*. 11 vols. New York: Charles Scribner's Sons, 1964.

Jones, Billy Mac. *Health-Seekers in the Southwest, 1817–1900*. Norman: University of Oklahoma Press, 1967.

Jordan, Weymouth T. *Ante-Bellum Alabama: Town and Country*. Florida State University Studies 27, 1957.

Kasson, John F. *Rudeness and Civility: Manners in Nineteenth-Century Urban America*. New York: Hill & Wang, 1990.

Lazenby, Marion Elias. *History of Methodism in Alabama and West Florida*. N.p.: North Alabama Conference and Alabama-West Florida Conference of the Methodist Church, 1960.

Levine, Lawrence W. *Highbrow/Lowbrow: The Emergence of Cultural Hierarchy in America*. Cambridge: Harvard University Press, 1988.

Longstreet, Stephen. *Win or Lose: A Social History of Gambling in America*. New York: Bobbs-Merrill Co., 1977.

Mahoney, William James, Jr. *One Hundred and Fifty Years: A Sesquicentennial History of the First Presbyterian Church*. Montgomery: Brown Printing Co., 1974.

Marshall, James Williams. *The Presbyterian Church in Alabama*. Montgomery: Presbyterian Historical Society of Alabama, 1977.

May, Earl Chapin. *The Circus from Rome to Ringling*. New York: Duffield & Green, 1932.

Murray, Marian. *Circus! From Rome to Ringling*. Westport, Conn.: Greenwood Press, 1956.

Neeley, Mary Ann. *The Works of Matthew Blue, Montgomery's First Historian*. Montgomery: NewSouth Press, 2010.

Oakes, James. The Ruling Race: A History of American Slaveholders. New York: Alfred A. Knopf, 1982.

Osterweis, Rollin G. *Romanticism and Nationalism in the Old South*. New Haven: Yale University Press, 1949.

Ottenberg, June C. *Opera Odyssey: Toward a History of Opera in Nineteenth Century America*. Westport, Conn.: Greenwood Press, 1994.

Pivar, David J. *Purity Crusade: Sexual Morality and Social Control*. Westport, Conn.: Greenwood Press, 1973.

Posey, Walter Brownlow, ed. *Alabama in the 1830's As Recorded by British Travellers*. Birmingham-Southern College Bulletin 31, December 1938.

Preston, Katherine K. *Opera on the Road: Traveling Opera Troupes in the United States, 1825–1860*. Chicago: University of Illinois Press, 1993.

Reid, Avery Hamilton. *Baptists in Alabama: Their Organization and Witness*. Montgomery: Paragon Press for the Alabama Baptist State Convention, 1967.

Rosenzweig, Roy. *Eight Hours for What We Will: Workers and Leisure in an Industrial City, 1870–1920*. Cambridge: Cambridge University Press, 1983.

Rugoff, Milton, ed. *Encyclopedia of American Art*. New York: E. P. Dutton, 1981.

Ryan, Mary P. *Cradle of the Middle Class: The Family in Oneida County*, New York, 1790–1865. New York: Cambridge University Press, 1981.

Sellers, James Benson. *The Prohibition Movement in Alabama, 1702 to 1943*. Chapel Hill: University of North Carolina Press, 1943.

Simon, Hannah, ed. *The First 100 Years of Kahl Montgomery*. Montgomery: Paragon Press, 1952.

Skinner, Maud and Otis. *One Man in His Time: The Adventures of H. Watkins, Strolling Player, 1845–1863, From His Journal*. Philadelphia: University of Pennsylvania Press, 1938.

Sulzby, James F., Jr. *Historic Alabama Hotels and Resorts*. University: University of Alabama Press, 1960.

Toll, Robert C. *Blacking Up: The Minstrel Show in Nineteenth-Century America*. New York: Oxford University Press, 1974.

Vance, Rupert Bayless and Demerath, Nicholas J., eds. *The Urban South*. Chapel Hill: University of North Carolina Press, 1954; reprint ed., Freeport: Books for Libraries Press of Freeport, N. Y., 1971.

Vaughn, William Preston. *The Antimasonic Party in the United States, 1826–1843*. Lexington: University of Kentucky Press, 1983.

Walton, George Edward. *The Mineral Springs of the United States and Canada, with Analyses and Notes on the Prominent Spas of Europe, and a List of Sea-Side Resorts*. New York: D. Appleton & Co., 1873.

Watson, Charles S. *The History of Southern Drama*. Lexington: University Press of Kentucky, 1997.

West, Anson. *A History of Methodism in Alabama*. Nashville: Publishing House Methodist Episcopal Church, South, 1893; reprint ed., Spartanburg, S. C.: The Reprint Co., 1983.

Whitaker, Walter C. *History of the Protestant Episcopal Church in Alabama, 1763–1891*. Birmingham: Roberts & Sons, 1898.

Wiebe, Robert H. *The Opening of American Society*. New York: Alfred A. Knopf, 1984.

Williams, Benjamin Buford. *A Literary History of Alabama: The Nineteenth Century*. Cranbury, N. J.: Associated University Presses, 1979.

Woolston, Howard Brown. *Prostitution in the United States Prior to the Entrance of the United States into the World War*. Montclair, N. J.: Patterson Smith, 1969.

Wood, Mattie Pegues. *The Life of St. John's Parish: A History of St. John's Church from 1834 to 1955*. Montgomery: Paragon Press, 1955; reprint ed. with a 1990 supplement by J. Mills Thornton III; Montgomery: Black Belt Press, 1990.

Zboray, Ronald J. *A Fictive People: Antebellum Economic Development and the American Reading Public*. New York: Oxford University Press, 1982.

Articles and Pamphlets

Blumin, Stuart M. "The Hypothesis of Middle-Class Formation in Nineteenth Century America: A Critique and Some Proposals," *American Historical Review* 90 (April 1985): 299–338.

Clarke, Thomas H. "Montgomery," in *Northern Alabama: Historical and Bibliographical*. Edited by T. A. DeLand and A. Davis Smith. Chicago: Donohue & Henneberry, 1888, 574–93.

Flynt, J. Wayne. "Alabama," in *Religion in the Southern States: A Historical Study*. Edited by Samuel S. Hill. Macon: Mercer University Press, 1983.

Hardy, Stephen. "'Adopted by All the Leading Clubs': Sporting Goods and the Shaping of Leisure, 1800–1900," in *For Fun and Profit: The Transformation of Leisure into Consumption*. Edited by Richard Butsch. Philadelphia: Temple University Press, 1990, 71–101.

Johnson, Claudia D. "That Guilty Third Tier: Prostitution in Nineteenth Century American Theaters," in *Victorian America*. Edited by Daniel Walker Howe. Philadelphia: University of Pennsylvania Press, 1976, 111–20.

McConachie, Bruce A. "Pacifying American Theatrical Audiences, 1820–1900," in *For Fun and Profit: The Transformation of Leisure into Consumption*. Edited by Richard Butsch. Philadelphia: Temple University Press, 1990, 47–70.

McDaniel, Tennent L. *History of the Montgomery Fire Department, 1817–1926*. Montgomery: n. p., 1926.

Mellown, Robert O. "Mental Health and Moral Architecture." *Alabama Heritage* 32 (Spring 1994): 5–17.

Napier, John H. III. "Martial Montgomery: Ante-Bellum Military Activity." *Alabama Historical Quarterly* 29 (Fall and Winter 1967): 107–31.

Owen, Thomas M. "The Methodist Churches of Montgomery," Montgomery: Paragon Press, 1908.

Somers, Dale A. "The Leisure Revolution: Recreation in the American City, 1820–1920," *Journal of Popular Culture* 5 (Summer 1971): 125–47.

Williams, Clanton Ware. "Early Ante-Bellum Montgomery: A Black Belt Constituency," *Journal of Southern History* 7 (November 1941): 495–525.

Dissertations and Theses

Fundaburk, Emma Lila. "Business Corporations in Alabama in the Nineteenth Century." 3 vols. Ph.D. dissertation, Ohio State University, 1963.

Owsley, Frank Lawrence, Jr. "Albert J. Pickett: Typical Pioneer State Historian." Ph.D. dissertation, University of Alabama, 1955.

Smith, Warren Irving. "Structure of Landholdings and Slaveownership in Ante-Bellum Montgomery County, Alabama." Ph.D. dissertation, University of Alabama, 1952.

Turnipseed, La Margaret. "The Ante-Bellum Theatre in Montgomery, Alabama, 1840–1860." M.A. thesis, Auburn University, 1948.

Wible, Hazel Butler. "History of Montgomery, Alabama, 1860–1865." M.A. thesis, Auburn University, 1939.

Williams, Clanton Ware. "History of Montgomery, Alabama, 1817–1846." Ph.D. dissertation, Vanderbilt University, 1938.

Young, Hugh Peter. "A Social and Economic History of Montgomery, Alabama, 1846–1860." M.A. thesis, University of Alabama, 1948.

Index

A

abolition 72, 100
Adrian, Adolphe 92
agriculture 3, 7, 73
Alabama General Assembly 35
Alabama Insane Hospital 35
Alabama Journal 70, 73, 79, 83
Alabama River 5, 21, 30, 65, 92, 97
Alabama's military act of 1860 42
Alabama State Agricultural Society Fair 46
Allen and Boothly Troupe 94
Amazon 82
American Art-Union 46
American Lyceum 32
American Sunday School Union 91
Apollonicon 84, 85, 86
Arnold, Herman Frank 76, 96
art exhibits 46
assemblies, grand balls 51–52
   Firemen's 76
   slave 52
associations, volunteer 30–39, 100
Audubon, John James 29
Augusta 43, 65

B

Bachelor's Club 31
balls, assemblies 51–52
   Firemen's 76
   slave 52
Baptist Church 59, 71, 104, 105, 110, 118, 120
Barnum, Phineas T. 89–90, 94
Barnum's Grand Scientific and Musical Theatre 90
Battle of Thlonotosassa Creek 41
Benedict Club 31
Benson, Nimrod E. 67
Benton 57
Bertrand [race] Course 57, 58, 59, 60
billiards 18, 20, 22
Bishop, Anna Reviere 79
Bladon Springs 63
Blount Springs 62
boat racing 18
Bogue Homme 26
Booth, Edwin 75
Booth, John Wilkes 75, 76
boxing 18
Boy Minstrels of Mobile 94
brawling 17, 21, 65
Broadway Menagery 86
Brough, William 79
Buckingham, James S. 23, 35
Buckley Opera Troupe 81
Bugbee, Francis 32
Bull, Ole 81
Bunyan, John 46

C

Campbell Minstrels 74, 93, 94
Camp Owen 43
Carter, David H. 57
Carter [race] Course 57–58, 60
Catherwood, W. C. 34
Cedar Hotel 63
Chang and Eng 90
Charleston 56, 57, 58, 65, 66, 79, 80, 95
Chevra Mevacher Cholim (synagogue) 11
Childs, Enoch 32
Christmas 45, 49–50
Christy, George 95
churches, religion 35, 71, 72, 97, 98
Church, Frederick Edwin 46
circuses and menageries 78, 82–92, 97
Circus, People's 92
Civil War 9, 14, 15, 38, 43, 76

125

Clayton, J. 83
climate, weather 65, 73, 75
Cline Brothers 89
Cobbs, Nicholas Hamner 13
cockfighting 17, 18, 65
Columbus 42, 65
commercial entertainment 14, 18, 35, 44, 65–97, 100
Commercial Hall 74, 89
Concert Hall 36, 75, 94
Confederates, Confederacy 3, 101
cotton 7, 73
Cowbellians 50
Crescent City Circus 86, 87
Crisp and Canning's Gaiety Theatre 74
Crisp, William H. 73, 75, 94
Cropsey, Jasper Francis 46
Cult of Chivalry 34, 39, 49, 99
Cushman, Charlotte 78

D

Dallas County 57
dancing, dancers 13, 51–53
Davis, Jefferson 96
DeBow's Review 91
Democratic State Convention 94
Den Stone's Circus 85–86, 87
de Vries, Madame Rosa 79
Dexter Fire Company 44
diseases 13, 73
Dix, Dorothea Lynde 35
"Dixie" 96
drinking 17, 22–25
 and alcoholic beverages 23
 and control of 24
 and slaves 23–24
 and temperance 24–25
Duffield Company 74

E

East Alabama Town 4, 5
Eldred, GN 87
Emma Waller 75
Emmett, Daniel 96
Episcopalians 12–13

everyday pastimes 13, 15–44
 drinking 15–17, 22–24, 65, 99
 fishing, angling 27–28, 30, 99
 gambling 15, 18–22, 65, 99
 hunting 27–28, 99
Exchange Hotel 73, 79, 94
exhibits, art 46

F

Fain's Tavern 19
fairs, fairgrounds 46–48, 54
farmers 9, 45, 46, 56
Federal Road 4, 65, 98
Feron, Elizabeth 78–79
Feron, Madame Anna 69
fire companies 43–44
 Dexter Fire Company 44
fishing, angling 27–28, 30
Fitzpatrick, Benjamin 67
foot racing 18
Fourth of July 42, 45, 53–54, 99
Fowler, Lorenzo Niles 34
Franklin, Benjamin 53
Franklin Society 31
Freemasons 37–38, 39, 53, 67
French Benevolent Society 11, 108

G

gambling 15, 17, 18–22
 and slaves 23
Gamester, The 20
gender roles 8, 15, 16, 26, 31, 67, 70, 94, 100
Gentry, the 21
George Christy's Minstrels 95
German Odd Fellows Lodge 11
Glidden, George R. 33
Godey's Lady's Book 53
Goldthwaite, Henry 67
Goliad 21
Gosse, Philip Henry 29
Grande Armanxa 84
Grand Lodge of Alabama 38, 39, 67, 109, 118
Great Southern Circus and Menagerie 88

H

Harper's Weekly 80
Hart, W. R. 72–73, 93
Hastings, Edmund McCurdy 41
Hayneville 57, 71
Henry, H. W. 41
Herr Ryninger 89
Hilliard, Henry 32
Hole in the Wall, Jr. 22
holidays 45–55
horse racing 15, 18, 55–61, 65, 100
hotels 68, 69, 89
    Exchange Hotel 73, 79, 94
Hundley, Daniel R. 27
Hunter, L. W. 60
hunting 27–30
Huntington, Daniel 46

J

Jackson, Andrew 53
Jennings, Ben 84
Jews 11, 44
John Brown's Raid 42
Johnson and Company's People's Circus 84

K

Knox, William 48
Kossuth, Louis 34

L

LaGrange, Georgia 42
Leati Operatic Group 79
lectures 31–37
leisure activities
    and elite 15, 18
    and epidemics 13
    and population 9
    and religion 11, 12–13, 17–18, 31, 91, 97
    and Sabbath 17–18, 24
    and slaves 8, 23–24
    and social values 4, 13, 31
    and socioeconomics 9, 13, 23, 33, 67, 75
    and weather 13
    and women 7, 14, 16, 30, 34
    appropriateness of 17, 30, 31, 66, 70–72, 91–92, 97, 99
Lemanski, Charles 34
Lever, Charles 49
LeVert of Mobile, Miss 48
libraries 31–32
Library Association 31
Lind, Jenny 78
Linn, Charles 54
Lipscomb, Andrew A. 31, 32, 33
Literary Club of Montgomery 34
literary societies 31–35, 100
lotteries 13, 18–20, 19, 20
Lowndesboro 57
Ludlow, Noah Miller 68–69, 73
Lyceum 31, 32, 33, 36

M

Mabie's Menagerie 85, 86, 87
Macon 42, 53, 65
manufacturing 7, 98
Market Street 42
marksmanship 28–29, 30
Masonic Signet 38
Masons. *See* Freemasons
Matthew, Theobold 24
May, John 84
McLeod, J. R. 92
Mechanics Association 33, 36
menageries 73
Mercy's Dream 46
Methodists 12, 38, 71
Metropolitan Guards 39–40
Mexican War 41–42
middling classes 10, 14, 15, 17, 33, 98, 99
militia 40, 42
mineral springs 7, 62–64
minstrel shows, minstrels 73, 78, 92–97
Mitchell, Maggie 75, 76
Mobile 5, 7, 22, 23, 33, 48, 50, 56, 58, 59, 63, 65, 69, 73, 78, 79, 85, 93, 98

Monsieur Paul 89
Montgomery
  and communications 98
  and Confederates capital 3
  and map 5
  as transportation center 7
  churches, religion 11–13, 17, 24–25
  class structure of 9–11, 14, 25, 27, 31, 75, 78, 95, 98, 100
  descriptions of 3, 17, 68, 75, 98
  economy of 7–8, 8–11, 73, 74, 81, 92
  education of 98
  history of 4–7, 21
  ordinances of 18, 20–21, 22–23, 25–26, 67, 88
  population of 7–9, 33, 45
Montgomery Advertiser 86
Montgomery Hall hotel 42, 79
Montgomery Jockey Club 57, 60, 61
Montgomery Lyceum 32, 33
Montgomery Theatre 75–76, 96
Montgomery Weekly Advertiser 76
Montgomery Weekly Post 60, 75, 76, 106, 107, 109, 110, 111, 112, 115, 117, 119
Mooney, Kenyon 21
Moore, Edward 20
Moore, Joseph Thoits 42
Moses Collier and Company 68
Mount Meigs 56
Mount Meigs Cavalry 42
music 16, 18, 78

N

New England 11
New Orleans 7, 33, 53, 58, 63, 65, 66, 68, 69, 73, 78, 79, 93
New Orleans English Opera Company 80
New Orleans Minstrel Troupe 95
New Philadelphia 4, 5, 11
New Year's 45, 50–51, 99
New York Knickerbocker Brass Band 84
night slave patrol 21

Nixon's Royal Circus 89
North American Circus 84

O

Odd Fellows 11, 37, 38, 39
Olmsted, Frederick Law 52, 82
open house, New Year's 50–51
opera 74, 78–82
operatic burlesque 81

P

Panic of 1837 72
parades 53
Parodi Italian Opera Company 81
pastimes, everyday 15–44
Patti, Amalia 81
Pensacola 63
Pentland, Joe 90
People's Circus 92
phrenology 34, 35
Piccolomini, Mariette 81
Pickett, Albert James 17, 62, 103, 105
Pickett, Eliza Goddard Whitman 12
Pilgrim's Progress 46
planters 9, 10, 11, 22, 33, 34, 44, 52, 56
pop calls, New Year's 50–51
population/demographics 9–11
Power, Tyrone 22
Prattville 7, 9
Presbyterian Church 12, 51, 71, 106, 111, 118
prostitution 17, 23, 25–27, 70, 75
Protestant 11–13, 44, 51

R

racial distinctions 75, 77, 78, 84, 90, 93, 94
Ramsey and Newcomb's Minstrels 95
Raymond's Menagerie 84
religion 11–13, 17, 66, 68, 72, 91
resorts. *See* mineral springs
revivals 12, 17, 72
Robinson, Cornelius 60
Robinson Springs 62
Roman Catholics 12, 44, 50

Russell, William Howard 3, 8, 101

S

Sabbath observances 17–18, 68, 83, 88
Sable Melodists 93
Sanford, Sam 94, 95
Sanford's Opera Troupe 94
Saratoga, New York 25
Savannah 65, 79
Sayre, Daniel 67
Scott, John 71
seasonal amusements and diversions 45–55, 81, 82, 94
    Alabama State Agricultural Society Fair 46–49
    Christmas 49, 57, 99
    Fourth of July 42, 45, 53–54, 99
    New Year's 50–51, 99
    summering at mineral springs 5, 62–64
    Thanksgiving 45, 49
Second Great Awakening 12, 17
Shakespeare 67–68, 77, 93, 97
Signor Donetti's troupe 89
slavery, slaves 4, 7, 9, 10, 23–24, 25, 34, 82, 91, 93, 94
    and insurrection 52–53
Smith, Sol 69, 70, 71, 72
Societies, secret fraternal 37–39
    and Masons. *See* Freemasons
    Odd Fellows 38–39
Southern Commercial Convention 94
Southern Female College 43
Southern Minstrels 95
Spaulding, Dr. 84
Spaulding & Roger's Floating Palace 84, 85
Spirit of the Times 56, 57, 60–61
sports 14
State Gazette 86
steamboats 5
    and passengers 22–23
Steyermarkesch Band 93
St. Paul's Encampment 38
Strikers 50

T

Talladega Springs 62
team sports 14
temperance
    American Temperance Society 24
    Orion 25
    Sons of Temperance 25
    Southern Times 25
    Temperance Society 24
    Washingtonian Society 24
Thalberg, Sigismund 81
Thanksgiving 45, 49
theater 15, 66–78. *See* Montgomery Theatre
    building 73–74, 75–76
    circuits 65, 69
    public attitude towards 70–72
The Gamester 20
Thespian Society 67, 68, 69, 72
Thlonotosassa Creek, Battle of 41
Thorington, John 21
Ticknor, Isaac 21
Tom Thumb 90
tournaments, tilts 47, 48–49
Towns, George W. B. 67
trade with China 35
transportation 5, 7, 13, 32, 35, 45, 63, 68, 84, 98
Tuscaloosa 35, 38, 69
Tyler's Indian Exhibition 85, 86, 87
Typographical Society 53

U

Uncle Tom's Cabin
    parodies of 77, 94, 95
Universalists 12

V

Valhermoso Springs 63
Van Amburgh, Isaac 86
Van Amburgh's Zoological Show and Circus 86
Van Deussen minstrels 79
Vaughan Family Troupe 68
Victoria, Queen 86, 88, 90

Vieuxtemps, Henri 81
violence 17, 21
Virginia Minstrels 95
volunteer fire companies. *See* fire companies
volunteer military companies 39–42, 53, 54, 100
    Alabama Dragoons 42
    and Columbus, LaGrange, and Macon companies 42, 53
    Henry's Horse Company. *See* Montgomery Huzzars
    Metropolitan Guards 39–40, 42
    Montgomery [County] Invincibles 41, 42
    Montgomery Dragoons 42
    Montgomery Greys 42
    Montgomery Huzzars 41
    Montgomery Light Infantry 41
    Montgomery Rifle Corps 42
    Montgomery [True] Blues 30, 41, 42, 43
    Mount Meigs Cavalry 42
    Relief Volunteers 42
    Riflemen 42
    Rough and Ready Invincibles. *See* Montgomery [County] Invincibles

W

Waller, Daniel 75
Waller, Emma 75
Ward Theatrical Company 74
Waring and Raymond's Circus and Menagerie 83
Washington's Birthday 42, 53
Watkins, Harry 73
Watson, Hugh Park 60
weather 13
Welch and Nathan's National Circus 84
Wells, Samuel Roberts 34
Wetumpka 9, 71
Wetumpka Light Guards 54
Whitney, Asa 35
Wigfall, Louis Trezevant 2, 3, 101
William Wright's Huntsman's and Fisherman's Emporium 27
Woodruff, C. A. 35
work
    nature of 15
Wright's Huntsman's and Fisherman's Emporium 27

Y

Yancey, William Lowndes 30
"Yankee Town" 11. *See also* New Philadelphia
Yeaman's Circus 82
Young Men's Debating Society 31

Z

Zoological Institute 91

About the Author

Jeffrey Benton, a retired Air Force colonel, has taught history and English at the University of Maryland Far East Division, The Citadel, the Air War College, Auburn University Montgomery, Troy University Montgomery, and The Montgomery Academy. His research focuses on local history. He has written extensively on Montgomery and its environs, including more than two hundred newspaper articles. His books include: *A Sense of Place: Montgomery's Architectural Heritage, 1821–1951*; *The Very Worst Road: Travellers' Accounts of Crossing Alabama's Old Creek Indian Territory, 1820–1847*; and *They Served Here: Thirty-three Maxwell Men*.

He received his BA from The Citadel, as well as master's degrees in English, political science, and history from the University of North Carolina at Chapel Hill, Auburn University Montgomery, and Auburn University.

He and his wife, Karen, have two daughters, Caroline and Catherine.

www.ingramcontent.com/pod-product-compliance
Lightning Source LLC
Chambersburg PA
CBHW030141170426
43199CB00008B/163